Timely Themes *from* Astronauts to Whales

Beth Alley Wise

Troll Associates

Interior Illustrations by: Marilyn Barr

Copyright © 1992 by Troll Associates. All rights reserved.
Permission is hereby granted to the purchaser to reproduce,
in sufficient quantities to meet yearly student needs, pages bearing
the following statement: © 1992 by Troll Associates.

ISBN: 0-8167-2587-X

Printed in the United States of America.

10 9 8 7 6 5 4 3 2

Contents

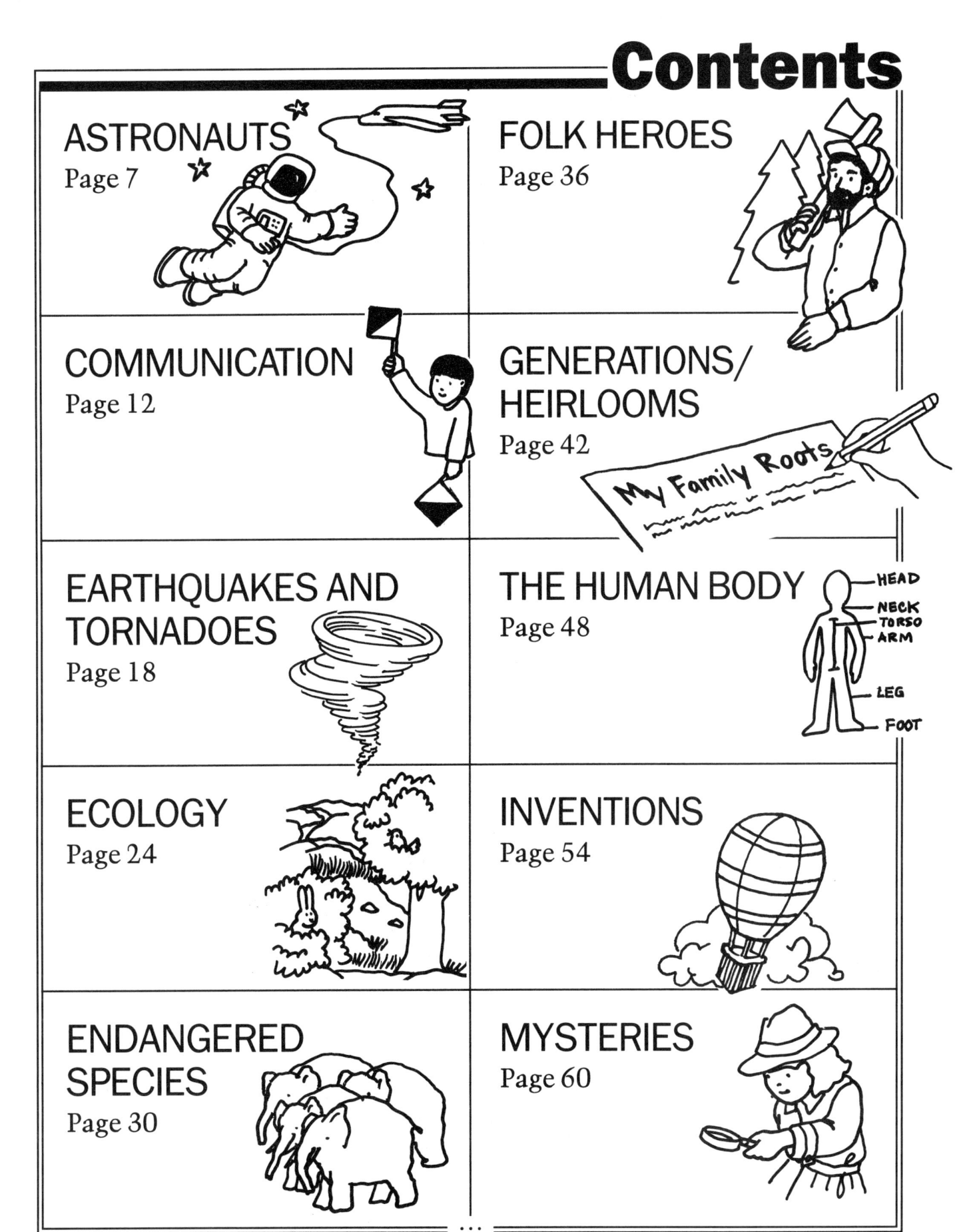

ASTRONAUTS
Page 7

COMMUNICATION
Page 12

EARTHQUAKES AND TORNADOES
Page 18

ECOLOGY
Page 24

ENDANGERED SPECIES
Page 30

FOLK HEROES
Page 36

GENERATIONS/HEIRLOOMS
Page 42

THE HUMAN BODY
Page 48

INVENTIONS
Page 54

MYSTERIES
Page 60

iii

THE OCEAN
Page 66

RECORDS
Page 72

THE SOLAR SYSTEM
Page 78

SURVIVAL
Page 84

WHALES
Page 90

Introduction

This book is filled with easy-to-do activities relating to topics that are among students' favorites. Whether they work in groups, in pairs, or alone, your students will enjoy themselves as they explore themes from astronauts to whales.

Each theme unit in this book contains a collection of activities from a variety of subject areas, including literature, ecology, science, and health. For example, your students will read folk tales and mysteries, plan a recycling program, experience the sensation of zero gravity, and observe and demonstrate basic first-aid techniques.

In addition to the kinds of activities suggested above, special activity sheets for each theme provide for fun and hands-on learning. For example, students will enjoy designing a spacesuit, encoding and decoding semaphore messages, devising a solar invention, creating a scrimshaw drawing, and much, much more.

In short, *Timely Themes from Astronauts to Whales* provides students with a fun-filled way to explore a wide range of topics that are sure to capture and hold their attention.

Astronauts

Gravity

Experiment with gravity. Hold a chalkboard eraser out in front of you. Let students predict what will happen when you let go of the eraser. Then drop it. Have students explain why the eraser fell to the ground instead of being drawn toward the ceiling or remaining suspended in space. If necessary, remind them that *gravity* is the force that draws objects toward the center of the earth.

The Ups and Downs of Weightlessness

Remind students that during a space flight the astronauts experience *zero gravity*, a state in which gravity is not present. Lead students in a discussion of the advantages and disadvantages of weightlessness during a space flight.

Training for Zero Gravity

Tell students that under zero gravity simple activities can become frustrating. As an example, point out that in zero gravity objects do not stay in one place when released but instead float away. Also, liquids do not pour but float out of their containers and into the air. Explain to students that in order to learn how to eat, drink, move, and work without the help of gravity, astronauts spend many hours in the zero-gravity chambers of the special *KC-135* jet.

A second part of zero gravity training is done in a water tank. Here astronauts learn to deal with the sensation of floating in space by putting on their spacesuits and performing their tasks under water.

Simple Chores Are Difficult

Let students experience the sensation of zero gravity by working in a mock training tank. Provide a large basin filled with water. Let students demonstrate each of the following tasks with their hands under water to find out which are easily performed and which are challenging.

1. Put toothpaste on a toothbrush.
2. Pour colored water or juice from one cup into another.
3. Pour dry cereal into a bowl.

Survival Training

Explain to students that astronauts undergo survival training in case a mishap occurs during a space flight and the crew must land somewhere other than the ocean or at one of the space centers. Two NASA Survival Schools, one deep in a jungle and one in the heart of a desert, teach astronauts how to make the best use of the equipment they have with them or can salvage from their wrecked spacecraft. Let students make a list of topics that might be taught in survival school. If they do not suggest the following, add them to the list:

jungle wildlife	how to make simple fish traps
how to find food	how to find water
which vegetation is edible	how to make tools or weapons
what danger lurks	how to find or make shelter
how to protect self from sun and cold	

Survival Kit

Tell students that each astronaut carries his or her own survival kit. The kit includes fishing lures and line, water purification tablets, burn ointment, food bars, soap, compass, small steel saw, sewing kit, antibiotic cream, desalting kit, pain killer, eyedrops, nose decongestant, and medicine for both diarrhea and nausea.

Have students imagine that they are astronauts on a spacecraft that made an emergency landing in a jungle. How could they use their survival kit when they got hungry? What in the kit could be used to treat injuries or minor illnesses?

Left High and Dry

Divide the class into five groups. Have students pretend that their spacecraft crashed into a jungle inhabited only by wild animals. After a close inspection, it is clear that the computers and the engines of the spacecraft are destroyed. However, other equipment or pieces from the spacecraft, space suits, and their survival kits are salvageable. Assign one of these topics at right to each group. Allow ample time to clarify the problem, discuss possible solutions, plan a strategy, list the materials needed and how to get or make them, and present their plan to the class. Encourage creative thinking and problem solving.

Group 1: Food and water
Group 2: Communication
Group 3: Transportation
Group 4: Shelter
Group 5: Protection

Eating in Space

Explain to students that preparing and eating food in space is a challenge. Food must be preserved to ensure that it does not spoil on a long trip, and it must be packaged so that it is easy to store, open, and eat in zero gravity. In addition, the food should taste good!

Tell students that many foods, such as hot dogs and hamburgers, are precooked and then put in aluminum bags. The astronaut opens the bag and eats the food right from the container. Explain that other foods are dehydrated and stored in plastic bags to save space. To return the foods to their original full-liquid state, astronauts use a device to squirt either hot or cold water into the bag.

Display dehydrated foods for students to observe and taste.

Space Drink

Let students make Space Juice. Have them measure and pour powdered drink mix into a glass, add the appropriate amount of cold water, and cover the glass with an airtight lid and shake.

Survival Mix

Dehydrate slices of apples, pineapple, and bananas by letting them dry in the sun. Add to the mixture any or all of the following ingredients: 1 cup (250 ml) raisins, 1 cup (250 ml) coconut flakes, 1 cup (250 ml) chocolate chips, and 3 cups (750 ml) mixed nuts. Mix and store in an airtight container for students to enjoy as a treat.

Stargazers

Explain that in order to verify their position in space, astronauts must learn to use the stars as points of reference. Tell students that astronauts are required to spend a great deal of time in the planetarium before they make their first space flight. It is in the planetarium that astronauts learn the names of the stars, the constellations, and the way they look at any season of the year and from any point along their space route.

Draw a constellation, such as the Big Dipper, on the chalkboard and identify it for students. Then point out its location in a summer sky and a winter sky. Have students discuss how knowing this information could help the astronauts navigate in space.

Rock Collectors

Tell students that astronauts must be able to recognize various types of rocks found on other planets, for this knowledge can help scientists learn how the other planets were formed. Ask students to find the definition for each of the following types of rocks, and to explain what scientists could learn about a planet if astronauts were to bring that kind of rock from its surface.

igneous rock rock formed by fire or great heat, especially by volcanic action

sedimentary rock rock formed by layers of sand, soil and shells that pile up layer upon layer

metamorphic rock rock that changed completely in form over a period of years

Rock Collections

Invite interested students to start rock collections. Suggest that they put the rocks in an egg carton or a cardboard box with dividers. Have them tell if the rocks are igneous, sedimentary, or metamorphic. Help students label the rocks.

Name _____ Date _____

Perfectly Suited

The only way to survive in space is to wear a good spacesuit. So the U.S. space agency is looking for the best suit possible for the astronauts who will be building the space station *Freedom* near the year 2000.

Here are spacesuits developed by two different companies. Look at the suits. Read about the advantages and disadvantages of each. Then *you* design a spacesuit for the *Freedom* astronauts to wear. Turn this paper over and draw a picture of your suit. Point out the features that make it better than the ones shown.

Advantage: The all-metal suit protects the astronaut from tiny meteors, radiation, and other space hazards.

Disadvantage: It weighs 185 pounds (84 km), which makes it hard to move in.

Advantage: This metal and fabric suit is light and easy to move in.

Disadvantage: The material might tear or puncture if hit by tiny space debris.

© 1992 by Troll Associates.

Communication

Computers Today

Explain to students that today's computers store information on chips, enabling them to process information in seconds. Tell students that these computers, called microcomputers, are very small compared to the room-sized computers used before 1960. Point out that many kinds of computers are used every day in and around the home and neighborhood. Have students suggest examples of common computers, such as a bar code scanner, gasoline pump, microwave oven, and video recorder/player. Have students make an inventory of computers in their school.

Computers Tomorrow

Tell students that today people can shop for many things by typing their orders into "smart computers" that think and reason on their own. Furthermore, the cost of the orders is deducted electronically from the purchaser's bank account. Discuss with students how computers of the future might take the process of buying goods one step further. For example, a computerized robot might deliver a person's order to his or her home. Then, if the person wants to return the goods for whatever reason, a robot might go back to the home to pick up the order.

Invite students to design a "smart computer" of their own. Ask them to explain how their computer would change people's lives.

Computer Languages

Tell students that communicating with a computer is like communicating with someone who does not speak the same language. A person must first learn the computer's language in order to "talk" to it. By learning the computer's language, a person can give "commands" to the computer. Invite interested students to find out more about these computer languages: BASIC, LOGO, DOS, PASCAL, COBOL, and FORTRAN.

Sign Language

Tell students that sign language is a language of gestures and hand symbols used by people who are hearing impaired. Explain that sign language was brought to the United States in the 1800s by Thomas Gallaudet. While sailing from France to the United States, Gallaudet met a teacher who taught him French sign language—a language in which the fingers are moved to positions that represent the letters of the alphabet. Once in the United States, Gallaudet opened a school for the deaf where he taught the language and added new signs that represented whole words and ideas.

Demonstrate to students signs that look very similar to the letters they represent, such as the signs for *o, c, v,* and *w.* Let students guess the letter for each sign.

Finger Talk

Make copies of the manual alphabet for students. Encourage students to study the alphabet carefully and then to practice signing to a friend. Remind them to position their hands so that they face toward the person reading the sign.

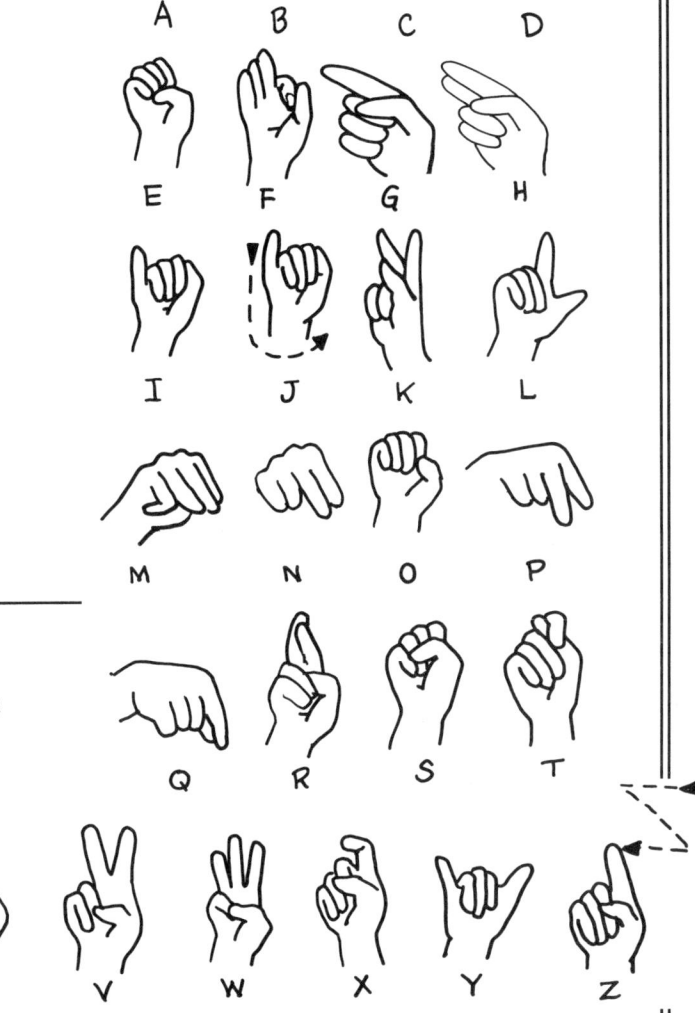

Underwater Language

Sign language has been used by the U.S. Navy frogmen to communicate under water. Have students brainstorm other occupations where using sign language might help people communicate more effectively. Have interested students write or call a local agency for the deaf to learn about situations other than signing for the deaf or hearing-impaired in which sign language is used.

Spelling Bee

Have a volunteer use the manual alphabet to spell the name of communication tools such as the telephone, telegraph, and the fax machine. Let the first student who identifies what has been spelled be the next speller.

Sports Charades

Play Sports Charades. Have students take turns acting out different sports. Explain that they may not use any verbal communication but only body language, including facial expressions, hand gestures, and body movements.

Sporting a New Language

Have students demonstrate signals that convey messages in other sports. Use a video recorder to tape the demonstrations. Edit the tape so that all signals for the same sport are grouped together. Then play the tape and have students guess the sport and the messages.

Sports Signals

Remind students that sports officials use body language to communicate information about the game to the players, coaches, and fans. Demonstrate or have volunteers demonstrate each of the signals for basketball and football shown here. Let students guess what information is being communicated.

FOOTBALL

1. Holding
2. Interference
3. Time out
4. Safety
5. Touchdown and field goal

BASKETBALL

1. Start the clock
2. Stop the clock
3. Traveling
4. Technical foul

14

Signs and Shapes

Divide the class into three groups. Assign each group a shape: circle, square, rectangle. Provide the groups with posterboard cutouts of their assigned shape. Instruct each group to make and display public signs that have that shape. Allow time for students to find signs in and around their neighborhoods to use as references. Post students' signs around the classroom.

Signs that Say "No"

Post the following signs. Point out that a sign with a red circle and a diagonal slash always means that something is prohibited. Let students paint their own signs using the circle and slash to illustrate class rules, such as NO GUM or NO RUNNING. Students may enjoy creating their own funny rules and signs to share with the class.

Logo Signs

Post some or all of these signs and explain that their purpose is to point to a service area or other important location. Have students locate important places around the school and help them make logo signs to help visitors find them more easily.

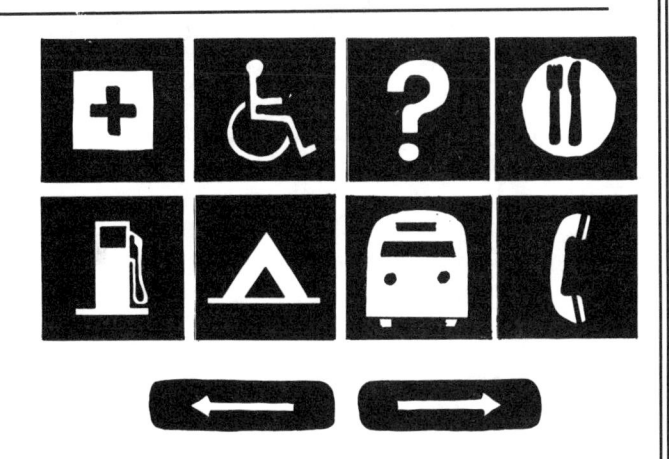

Answer to "Wave a Message": *Watch out for sharks!*

15

Wave a Message

Sailors, lifeguards, and others use a special language to communicate with people who are within seeing range but who are not within hearing range. The system, called semaphore, uses red and white flags held in different positions to represent each letter of the alphabet.

Study the alphabet. Then decode the message below.

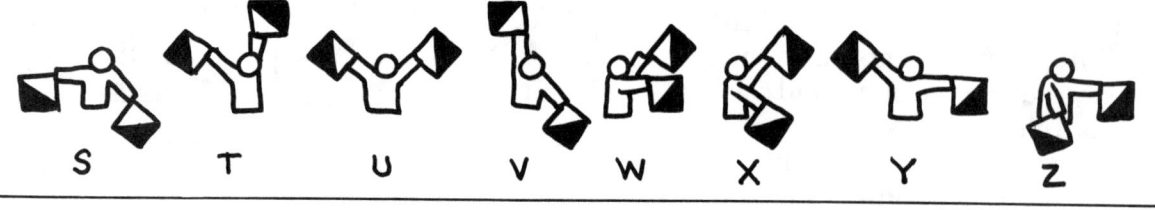

Make semaphore flags from cloth or poster board. Use the flags to "wave" a message of your own.

Name _____ Date _____

Time to Mime

Look at the pictures below. Write a brief description of the idea or feeling that each gesture expresses.

Hand Gestures

Face Gestures

_____ _____ _____ _____

Body Gestures

_____ _____ _____

Miming on Your Own

First pantomime each of the gestures suggested above. Then use a combination of hand, face, and body gestures to pantomime ordinary activities such as scolding a naughty puppy, catching a fish, picking a thorny rose, licking an ice cream cone, taking freshly baked cookies from the oven, or other activities of your choice. See how many people can guess your body language.

© 1992 by Troll Associates.

Earthquakes and Tornadoes

Earthquake!

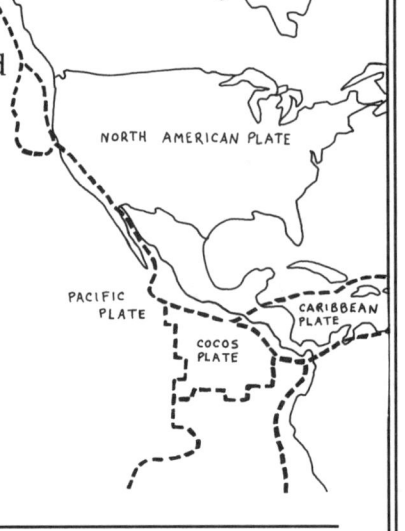

Explain that the earth's crust is made of thirteen large pieces called plates. Draw or trace lines on a map to show these four of the earth's plates: Pacific Plate, North American Plate, Cocos Plate, and the Caribbean Plate. Have students tell on which plate their home is. Then point to California on the map. Have students locate Los Angeles and San Francisco. Point out that the two cities are on two different plates. Explain that the plate on which Los Angeles rests is moving north and the plate on which San Francisco rests is moving south. Tell students that California has more than one hundred earthquakes a year, most of which are small. Explain that earthquakes happen when the plates shift against each other, causing the earth to shake and crumble.

Earthquake Protection

Have students discuss and demonstrate safety practices to protect themselves in the event of an earthquake.

PUT OUT FIRES   STAY INDOORS    COVER HEAD

San Andreas Fault

Tell students that a fault is a crack in the earth's crust. Then point out on a map the San Andreas Fault, explaining that it is the crack line between the two plates that divide California. Tell students that millions of years ago the part of California west of the fault was much farther south, probably where Mexico is today. Ask students to speculate where Los Angeles will be located a million years from now. Invite interested students to work together to make a map that shows past, present, and future locations of cities along the San Andreas Fault.

Richter Scale

Tell students that earthquakes are measured on a scale of magnitude, or extent of damage caused, and that this scale is called the Richter scale in honor of its creator, Dr. Charles Richter. The chart below is a simple outline of what the numbers on the scale mean. Copy the chart on the chalkboard. Distribute drawing paper to students and have them do pencil sketches to illustrate each level of magnitude.

Richter Scale	Level of Magnitude
1	Tremor recorded only by sensitive instruments.
2	A few people and animals feel tremor.
3	Tremors felt by most people.
4	All people feel rumbles. Lamps and pictures move.
5	Objects may fall off wall; vases may tumble over.
6	Walls crack. Stone structures may fall apart.
7	Landslides occur. Whole structures may crumble. Major earthquake.
8	Great earthquake. Buildings collapse.
9	Great earthquake. Massive destruction.
10	No earthquake has yet measured 10 on the Richter scale.

Major Earthquakes

Copy the following chart on the chalkboard. Have students complete the chart, filling in the dates, numbers on the Richter scale, and levels of damage.

Place: Alaska

Date: March 27, 1964

Richter scale: _____

Damage: The ground rose 50 feet (15 m), causing a 278-foot-high (85-m) wave.

Place: San Francisco, California

Date: October 17, 1989

Richter scale: _____

Damage: _____

Place: Iran

Date: June 21, 1990

Richter scale: _____

Damage: 40,000 people killed and 60,000 people injured

Place: China

Date: _____

Richter scale: _____

Damage: 830,000 people killed

Place: _____

Date: _____

Richter scale: _____

Damage: _____

Place: _____

Date: _____

Richter scale: _____

Damage: _____

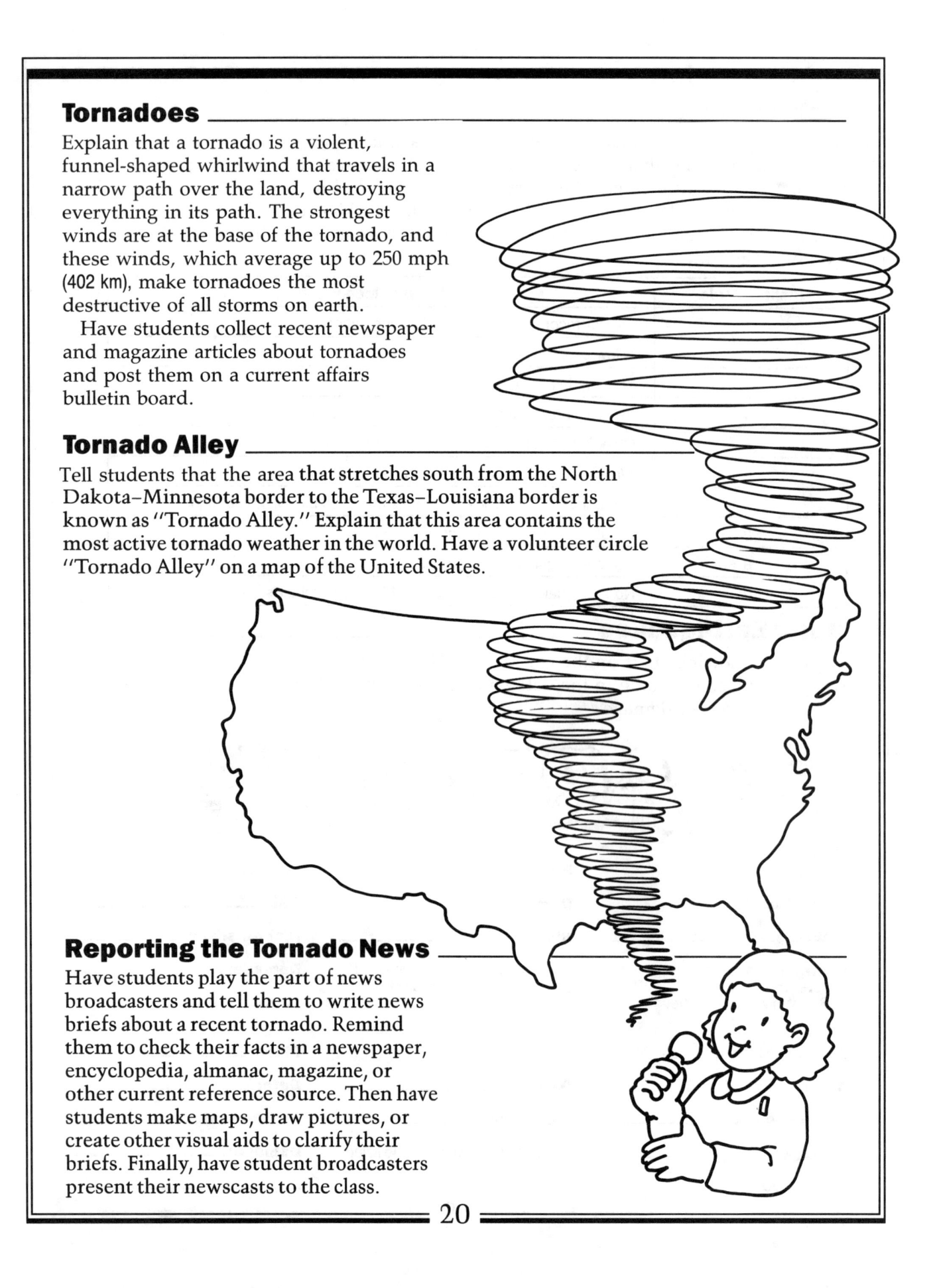

Tornadoes

Explain that a tornado is a violent, funnel-shaped whirlwind that travels in a narrow path over the land, destroying everything in its path. The strongest winds are at the base of the tornado, and these winds, which average up to 250 mph (402 km), make tornadoes the most destructive of all storms on earth.

Have students collect recent newspaper and magazine articles about tornadoes and post them on a current affairs bulletin board.

Tornado Alley

Tell students that the area that stretches south from the North Dakota–Minnesota border to the Texas–Louisiana border is known as "Tornado Alley." Explain that this area contains the most active tornado weather in the world. Have a volunteer circle "Tornado Alley" on a map of the United States.

Reporting the Tornado News

Have students play the part of news broadcasters and tell them to write news briefs about a recent tornado. Remind them to check their facts in a newspaper, encyclopedia, almanac, magazine, or other current reference source. Then have students make maps, draw pictures, or create other visual aids to clarify their briefs. Finally, have student broadcasters present their newscasts to the class.

Tornado Power

Make a tornado mobile. Cut a large funnel-shaped tornado from black poster board. From the tornado, hang poster board cutouts like the ones shown here. Write factual information about tornadoes on each piece. Have students read the information. Then encourage them to research, write, and add to the mobile other pieces of information about tornadoes.

In 1937 a tornado picked up a train locomotive, turned it around in the other direction, and put it down on another railroad track.

A tornado once pushed a string of railroad cars 25 miles before the cars could be stopped.

Tornadoes have scooped up ponds, then dropped them somewhere else. What would you think if you saw it "raining" frogs and fish?

A tornado in Kansas picked up a barbed-wire fence, rolled it up neatly, and then dropped it on the ground nearby.

During a tornado, wind drove a single piece of straw into a huge oak tree.

Tornado Conditions

Explain that scientists have determined the general conditions that create tornadoes. Tornadoes occur when warm, moist air meets cold, dry air. Violent weather is created at the front, or border, of these two kinds of air. As the winds push against each other, they begin to whirl. The whirling winds develop into a tornado.

Create a small tornado. Have students observe as you complete the procedure. Fill a jar with warm water. Use a very cold spoon to represent the jet stream (the cool, fast-moving winds high above the ground). Stir the water in a clockwise motion with the spoon. Observe the warm water and the cold spoon as they come in contact with each other. Watch as the water pushes and spins, forming a funnel cloud. Remove the spoon from the jar and watch how the "tornado" moves around in the jar. Repeat the experiment. This time, put three to four spoons of sand and a small plastic object, such as a counter, in the bottom of the jar before you begin. Students will be curious to find out what effect the "tornado" has on the sand and the object.

Weather Services

Tell students that there are thousands of "storm watchers" who look for severe weather all over the world. Explain that the United States has a special office in Kansas City, Missouri, that not only watches, but also warns people of threatening weather conditions. Tell students that this office, called the National Severe Storms Forecast Center (NSSFC), is where meteorologists, or weather scientists, use many tools to help them predict future tornadoes and earthquakes.

Weather Satellites
The satellites orbit thousands of miles (kilometers) above the earth, taking pictures of cloud formations and disturbances.

Radar Network
Radar signals bounce off raindrops and hail high in the sky, showing places where tornadoes may develop.

Hourly Observations
Observers all over the world send hourly reports to the NSSFC. The data may show conditions for a storm to develop.

Preparing for a Tornado

Have students make posters to show these steps for protecting themselves from a tornado.

AT HOME: Go into the basement or cellar beneath your house. If your house does not have an underground space, hide in a closet or bathroom in the middle of the house. Hide under a sturdy piece of furniture or a staircase and cover your head with pillows or a mattress.

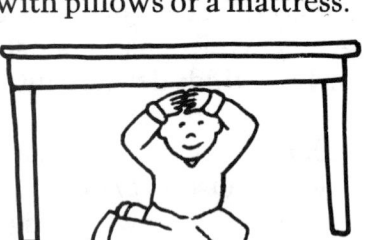

AT SCHOOL: Stay away from rooms with big windows and high ceilings that may cave in. Hide under a desk or table and cover your head with your hands.

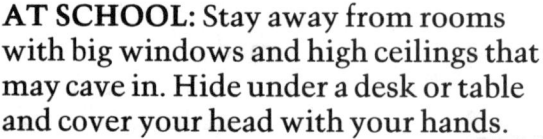

IN A CAR: Get out of the car and go into a building or lie down in a ditch and protect your head.

IN A MOBILE HOME: Leave at once. A tornado can easily destroy mobile homes or pick them up and drop them in another place!

22

Name _____ Date _____

Weather Word Watcher

Use the words in the box and the clues to complete the puzzle.

| predict | earthquake | plates | tornado | Richter | funnel |
| cellar | meteorologist | radar | satellite | eight | fault |

CLUES

ACROSS

4. Shaking of the ground caused by the shifting of underground rock
6. Great earthquake; buildings collapse
9. Underground room
11. Storm with a violent whirling column of air
12. Weather scientist

DOWN

1. A scale to measure the intensity of an earthquake
2. Rocky, puzzlelike pieces that make up the earth's crust
3. To tell what will happen before it happens
5. Instrument that takes pictures thousands of miles above the earth's surface
7. Shape of most tornadoes
8. Crack in the earth's crust
10. Instrument that bounces signals off rain drops to locate tornadoes

© 1992 by Troll Associates.

Ecology

Junk Jokes

Have students answer these jokes about junk.
- What do you call three feet of trash? *[a junkyard]*
- Why did the boy throw the letter out the window? *[He wanted to send it air mail.]*
- What has four wheels and flies? *[a garbage truck]*
- What do you call a wastebasket filled with clocks? *[a waste of time]*

Land Pollution

Explain to students that our land is becoming polluted, that is, beautiful green pastures, valleys, and other grasslands are being buried by heaps of trash or destroyed by chemicals. Our wasteful habits are causing a serious problem. Share these pollution facts with the students:

Americans throw away more trash than anyone else. In one year, Americans throw away enough trash to bury 1,000 football fields under a pile 300 feet (91½ m) deep!

People love burgers from fast-food restaurants, but the billions of burger boxes left behind each month could easily fill the Louisiana Superdome!

Americans throw away more than two billion batteries each year.

We could circle the Earth four times with the soda cans thrown away in just one week.

What a Bunch of Junk

Have students create a diagram on the chalkboard by writing the names of land pollutants. Then have them list alternatives to throwing away the litter and chemicals.

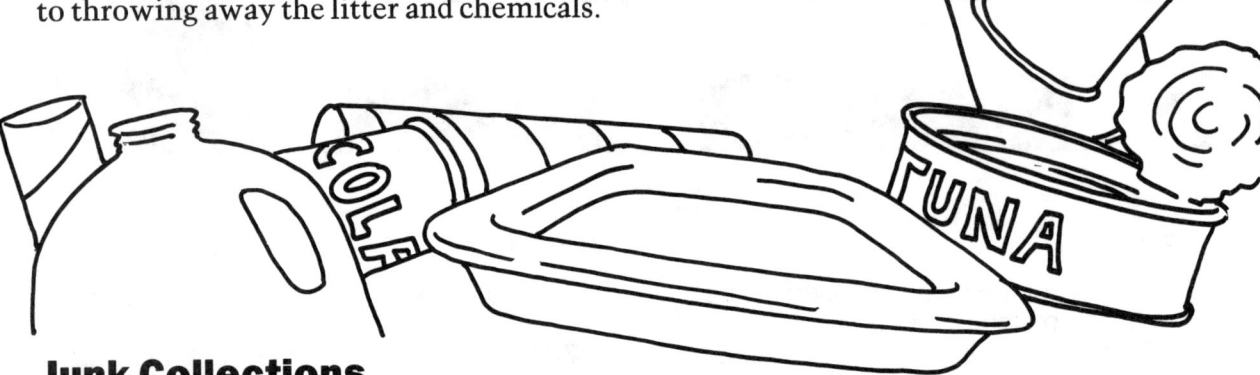

Junk Collections

Have students find out how many glass jars they throw away each week. Instruct students to collect the cap or lid from each glass bottle they discard. Tell students to do the following: At the end of one week, count the caps and lids. Multiply the number by fifty-two (number of weeks in a year) to find out the approximate number of glass jars discarded in one year.

Air Pollution

Explain that the earth is wrapped in a layer of usable air that is only 5 miles (8 km) high. Beyond that the air becomes thinner and thinner until it disappears. Tell students that we breathe the same air over and over again and that is why when we pollute our air supply, we experience breathing difficulties or, in extreme cases, death. Point out that humans are not the only ones affected by air pollution. All living things on earth, including plants and animals, are affected too.

Have students brainstorm things that pollute the air. List the responses on a chalkboard or a chart.

Gasoline Ghosts

Remind students that all gasoline engines cause air pollution. Copy the following chart on the board. Have students work in small groups to fill in the chart with the names of gasoline-powered engines . . . many of which can be found right around their homes.

••• GASOLINE-POWERED ENGINES •••

On the Street	In the Air	In the Garage	In the Backyard	In the Water
bus	jet	electric saw	power lawn mower	jet ski

Help Is on Its Way

Have interested students find out about the Clean Air Act. Have them report to the class about what the act says and how it helps fight air pollution.

Dirty Air

Help students do an experiment to discover the visible pollutants in the air.

YOU WILL NEED: a small glass jar, a large glass jar, white petroleum jelly

WHAT TO DO: Smear petroleum jelly on the small jar and then gently set it inside the large jar. Set the jars outside for a few days. Then have students observe the small jar. They will find that the petroleum jelly has picked up dirt carried by the air. Explain that what they see on the small jar is the result of air pollution alone, since the large jar will protect the small one from ground dirt and debris.

Water Pollution

Tell students that most people take water for granted even though in some places it is a diminishing resource. Share some of the water problems below.

- Accidents, such as oil spills, pollute our oceans and kill wildlife.
- Many household chemicals, such as paints, pesticides, and cleaners, get into the ground and then seep into the water and contaminate it.
- Many factories dump their toxic wastes into streams or rivers. These wastes get into our drinking water and cause people to become ill.

Waste Not

Have students make posters that show ways to conserve water. Some suggestions follow.

- Turn off water when not using it. A leaky showerhead can waste up to 20 gallons (75¾ L) a day. A leaky faucet wastes nearly 50 gallons (190 L) a day. Running the water while brushing your teeth may waste 5 gallons (19 L).
- Minimize water use. Sweep the driveway instead of hosing it down. Water the lawn at night so the sun doesn't dry up the water so fast. Refrigerate drinking water and boil cooking water instead of letting the faucet run until the water is the right temperature.

Pollution Solution

Tell students that cleaning up the water must begin at home and at school. Suggest to students that they start by using less toxic cleaners. Help students mix general cleaners that use safer chemicals.

ALL-PURPOSE CLEANER

Mix 2 teaspoons (10 ml) borax and 1 teaspoon (5 ml) biodegradable soap in one quart (1 L) water. Store in a spray bottle.

WINDOW-AND-MIRROR CLEANER

Mix 3 tablespoons (45 ml) white vinegar with 1 quart (1 L) warm water. Store in a spray bottle.

Clean up Your Act

State the problem: Millions of pounds of trash are being thrown out each day. Ask students to think of possible solutions to the problem. Encourage creative thinking. If students do not suggest the following solutions, provide them as possibilities for discussion: reducing the amount of trash thrown away, reusing things before finally throwing them away, and recycling items.

Recycle

Explain that *recycling* means to use waste material over and over again to conserve natural resources. For example, old paper can become new paper; old cans can become new cans, a new toy, or a new fork. The following are four basic materials that most local facilities can recycle: glass, plastics, paper, and metal. Have students interview the manager of your local solid-waste treatment plant to find out more about recycling in your area.

One Person's Trash, Another Person's Treasure

Have students imagine that they find something buried in a heap of garbage and that this thing turns out to be very valuable. Have them write a story describing the object and how they found it. Tell them to be sure to explain what the object is or will be used for and why the previous owner threw the object away.

Start a Recycling Program

Help students plan a recycling program for your school. You may wish to use some of the following suggestions to start your program:

- Gather four large cardboard boxes or plastic bins to collect the recyclable material.
- Label the boxes so students know what kind of material goes into each: GLASS, METAL, PAPER, and PLASTIC. Put the boxes in a place that is accessible but not obtrusive.
- Put the boxes out for curbside pick-up if your community has such a service, or organize a recycling pick-up day when a group of students and their parents take the boxes to the recycling center.
- Get everyone in the school involved: hand out posters around the school to tell about the recycling program, invite a local newspaper or TV station to announce your program, have a contest between individual classes or grade levels to see who can collect the most recyclable materials, and/or volunteer to help the cafeteria staff sort materials to be recycled.
- Make a chart to record the amount of materials sent to the recycling center each week. Read the results over the school intercom and post the chart where students can check their progress.
- Allow one day a week for teachers to "scrounge" through the bins, gathering materials for classroom art projects.

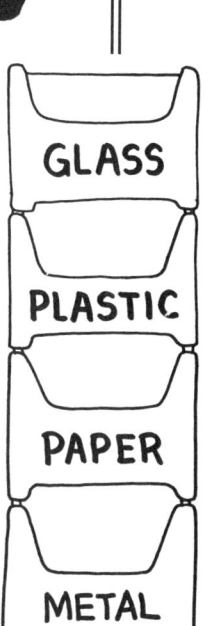

Name _____ Date _____

Dumper Stumper

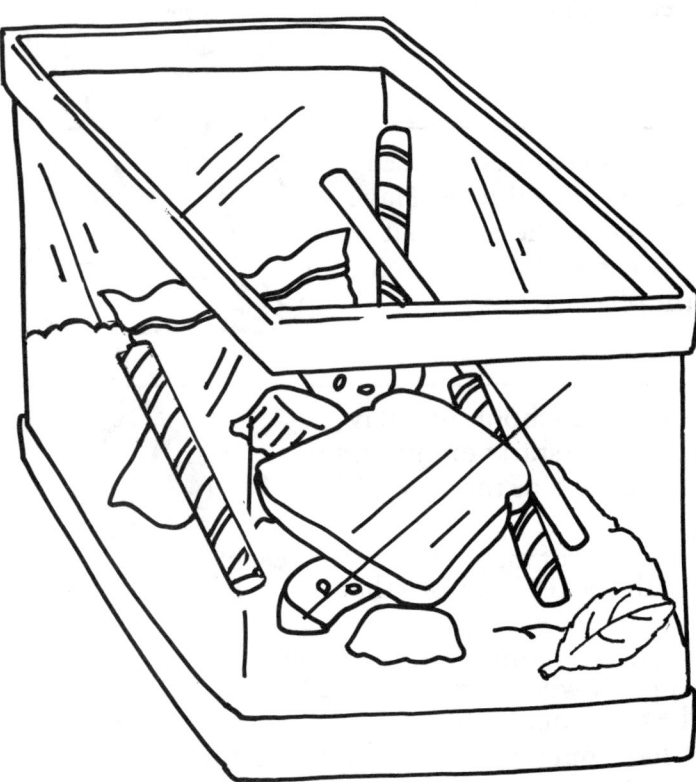

Which items do you think will break down or rot in the soil?

Color them.

Do this simple experiment to see if you are right. Make a minilandfill.

1. Get a large glass container such as an old fish tank or empty jar.
2. Fill the container with wet dirt. Put it in a warm place. (Keep the dirt very moist.)
3. Pile garbage (slices of apple, piece of bread, drinking straws, bottle cap, leaf, and plastic bag) in your minilandfill.
4. Watch what happens to the garbage in the landfill every day for a month. Write down any changes that occur to the garbage.
5. At the end of the month, dig through the garbage. Look to see which items rotted and became part of the soil. Did you guess correctly?
6. Draw the objects that did *not* break down. Think about them the next time you send garbage to the landfill.

EARTH ENEMIES

© 1992 by Troll Associates.

Name _____ Date _____

Recycled Bird Feeder

Use a discarded milk carton to make a bird feeder.

You will need:

discarded milk carton
hole punch
heavy string or wire
scissors
pencil
grass
twigs
birdseed
bread crumbs

1. Cut out a large hole on one side of the milk carton.

2. Punch two holes in the top of the carton. Thread string or wire through the holes and tie. Use this to hang the feeder from a tree.

3. Place some grass and twigs in the feeder. Add some birdseed or bread crumbs.

4. Listen to the birds as they come to the feeder. They may be thanking you.

© 1992 by Troll Associates.

Endangered Species

Tell students that in every corner of the world animals are being killed by people. Explain that many animals are killed for their skins, feathers, horns, or tusks, and many animals die when the land where they find their food and build their homes is torn down to build factories or highways. In addition, some animals are killed by accident, while others are hunted or killed for sport. Tell students that unless the killing stops, many kinds of animals will vanish forever from the earth.

Have students draw and label or cut out from magazines pictures of endangered animals. Post the pictures on a "Disappearing Animals" bulletin board.

African Elephant

Display a picture of an African elephant and explain to students that in the last ten years, more than half of their population has disappeared from the earth—so many, in fact, that experts are worried that they might become extinct. Explain that this tragedy happens because people want to buy ivory statues, jewelry, and other decorative items, so hunters kill thousands of elephants, remove their tusks, and sell the ivory to artists who create the decorative items. These artists or their agents then sell the items to people who want objects made of ivory.

National Symbol

Ask students to name the animal that was chosen as the national symbol of the United States. Explain that the bald eagle was chosen because it symbolizes strength and freedom. Display a coin or a piece of paper money with the bald eagle visible on it. Have students find other objects that contain an eagle. Some examples include stamps, flagpoles, jewelry, presidential limousine or jet, lecterns, logos on chip bags, aluminum cans, and Frisbees. Point out that you can find the eagle almost everywhere except where it truly belongs—flying freely.

Endangered Eagles

Remind students that although eagles once flew freely across the United States and Canada, they are now on the endangered list in both countries. Four reasons account for the majority of the devastation: pollution, pesticides, destruction of their habitats, and outright killing of these birds. Today, there are laws to protect the eagles. Have students contact the National Wildlife Federation, a state or local wildlife conservation group, or your librarian to find out the penalty for possessing eagle feathers, molesting eagles, or killing them.

Eagle Nests

Tell students that bald eagles usually build their nests in the tops of large trees. Most eagles return year after year to the same nests, adding twigs and sticks on each visit. A new nest must accommodate the adult eagle, which will likely weigh more than 25 pounds ($11\frac{1}{3}$ kg) and have a 7-foot ($2\frac{1}{8}$-m) wingspan. Students will be interested to know that one nest in Florida had been used for thirty-four years and was nearly 15 feet ($4\frac{1}{2}$ m) in diameter and weighed an estimated 2 tons (1.8 metric tons)!

Have students use sticks and twigs to build a nest 15 feet ($4\frac{1}{2}$ m) in diameter. Let students experiment to see how many of them can fit into the nest at one time. Then leave the nest in the schoolyard and see if eagles or other animals "move in."

Manatee Malice

Display pictures of manatees in their natural environment and explain that manatees are large, gray-brown, aquatic mammals. Tell students that although these plant-eating, slow-moving, air-breathing mammals were once plentiful, there are fewer than 1,200 remaining in the United States today. Because the manatee is harmless and defenseless, its worst enemies are humans. Careless boaters, canal locks, barges, crab traps, and fishing lines injure or kill the animals as they graze along shallow grass beds.

Have students research the manatee and explain how it is suited to its aquatic life. Then let students think of ways the manatee could be better adapted to its habitat.

Manatee Deaths

Reproduce the graph shown here. Have students study the graph to determine the major causes of manatee deaths. Ask students to suggest guidelines for protecting these peaceful creatures.

Natural Causes:
- Unusually cold weather
- Red tide (water colored by poisonous marine organisms)

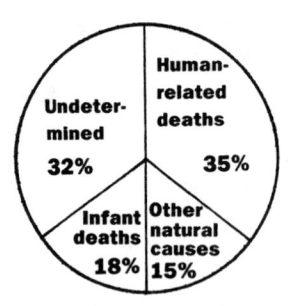

Undetermined 32%
Human-related deaths 35%
Infant deaths 18%
Other natural causes 15%

Human-Related Mortality:
- Loss of habitat
- Boat and barge collisions
- Crushed or drowned in floodgate or canal lock
- Pollution
- Other—fishing line, litter, hunting, harassment

Adopt a Manatee

As a class project, you may want to "adopt" a manatee. By doing so, students will learn and help others be informed about the manatee's plight and what they can do to ensure its survival. Your support of the Save the Manatee Club will provide manatee warning signs near their water homes and will help to ensure the safety of manatee habitats so that this gentle mammal can live undisturbed and free. As "parents," your class will receive adoption papers, photos, and biographical information about its adopted manatee, as well as fact sheets, newsletters, and other information about manatees in general. (There is a small adoption fee that a parent or interested citizen may be willing to pay, or students may collect the fee as a class project.)

For more information, write to:
Save the Manatee Club,
500 N. Maitland Ave., Maitland, FL 32751

Gray Whale

The gray whale has brushlike strainers instead of teeth. It gulps a mouthful of water, then squirts the water through the strainers. When the water is gone, the whale is left with a heap of fish for its dinner.

Gray whales often carry thousands of "passengers" on their backs. These passengers, called barnacles, attach themselves to the whales' skin and eat tiny organisms off the whales' bodies.

Share with students the facts below about the gray whale. Then encourage students to write books that include other whale facts. Some suggestions are:

1. How the gray whale evolved from a land animal into a sea animal.
2. Blubber—why they have it and why hunters kill for it.
3. How gray whales communicate with one another.
4. The size of gray whales compared to the sizes of other animals.
5. How much the gray whale eats in a day.

The Hunt Goes On

Tell students that marine mammals are hunted commercially for their meat, blubber, and skin. Many species of whales, including the gray whale, blue whale, bowhead whale, finback whale, and humpback whale are now considered endangered, due largely to this hunting.

Read to the students the following excerpt from the Endangered Species Act. Briefly discuss with them both sides of the issue: Wildlife conservationists are pleased that a law to protect the whale exists; people who make their living by hunting the whales and people who make products from the whales' blubber are not pleased by the law. Let students choose sides: those who think the law should be repealed and those who think the law should be upheld. Ask students to research, plan, and debate the law as it applies to killing whales. Allow five to six minutes for each side to present its case, three minutes for each to present its rebuttal, and another minute for closing statements.

The Endangered Species Act

"... it is illegal to kill, hunt, collect, harass, harm, pursue, shoot, trap, wound, or capture" a member of an endangered species.

Answers to Activity Sheet: wax, soap, lipstick, shampoo, margarine; whales

Name _____ Date _____

Battle for Blubber

Complete the name of each product shown.

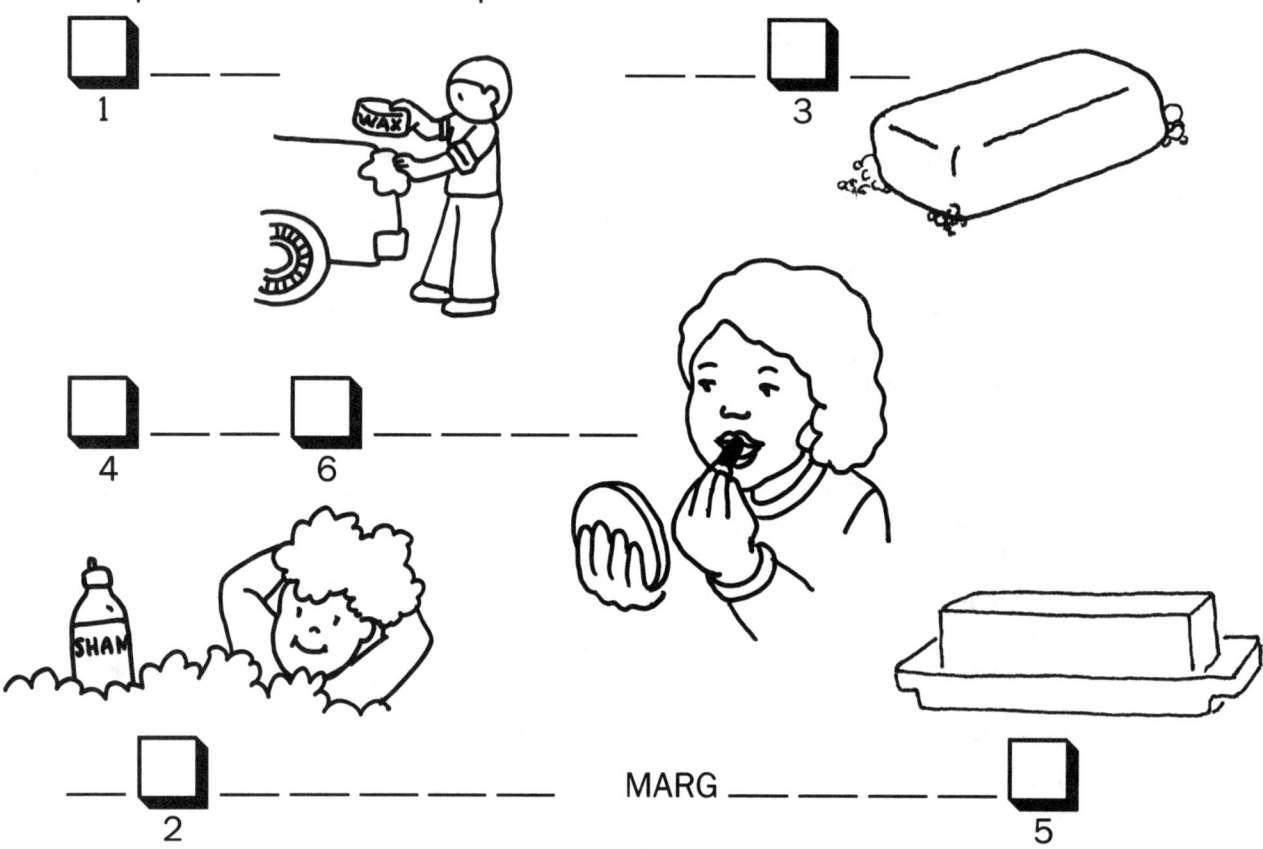

☐ __ __ __
1

__ __ ☐ __ __
3

☐ __ ☐ __ __ __ __ __ __
4   6

__ ☐ __ __ __
2

MARG __ __ __ __ ☐
5

Use the boxed letters from the puzzle above to discover the name of one animal that is slaughtered so that people can have household products made from its blubber.	Oil from the jojoba bean can be substituted for whale oil. Find two examples of household products that use jojoba bean instead of whale oil. Draw pictures of the products here.

1	2	3	4	5	6

Draw the animal.

34

© 1992 by Troll Associates.

Name _____ Date _____

A Lighter Look

Look at the cartoon below. It shows a very real problem—elephants being killed so people can use their tusks to make decorative ivory objects. Notice how the artist uses a cartoon to make a serious point in a simple, direct way.

Draw cartoons that make a serious point in a humorous way.

Serious point: Tortoise shell is used to make combs, mirrors, sunglasses, and other items. Tortoises are now endangered.

Serious point: Crocodiles are killed by the thousands largely because their skins make attractive handbags, watchbands, and shoes.

© 1992 by Troll Associates.

Folk Heroes

Folk Tales
Remind students that *folk tales* are stories handed down orally from generation to generation. The folk heroes that follow are characters from some well-known folk tales.

Paul Bunyan
Tell students that Paul Bunyan was the biggest, strongest, toughest logger who ever lived, and that at birth, he weighed an incredible 86 pounds (39 kg)! When he was full grown, he was taller than the tallest pine tree.

Tell students a bit about Paul Bunyan's life. He began logging in Maine and was so fast with his axe that he cut down all the trees in that state. Paul then moved west and settled near the Onion River. There, with his blue ox, Babe, Paul hired a crew of very tall, very strong, and very hungry men to help with his work. When the men sat at the dinner table, the line was so long and the tables were so big, that the women who served the meals had to wear roller skates to get from one end to the other. And no amount of drinks could satisfy the crew's thirst until Paul Bunyan himself dug the Great Lakes so his men could have plenty of drinking water.

Tales About Paul Bunyan
Have students read complete versions of Paul Bunyan and his adventures. Some suggested books follow.
Kellogg, Steven. *Paul Bunyan: A Tall Tale.* Morrow, 1984.
Lyman, Nanci A. *Paul Bunyan.* Troll, 1980.
Rounds, Glen. *The Morning the Sun Refused to Rise: An Original Paul Bunyan Tale.* Holiday House, 1984.
———. *Ol' Paul: The Mighty Logger.* Holiday House, 1976.

Share a Tall Tale
Invite students to share their favorite tale about Paul Bunyan. Have them draw a picture of Paul to go along with their story.

Steel-Drivin' Man

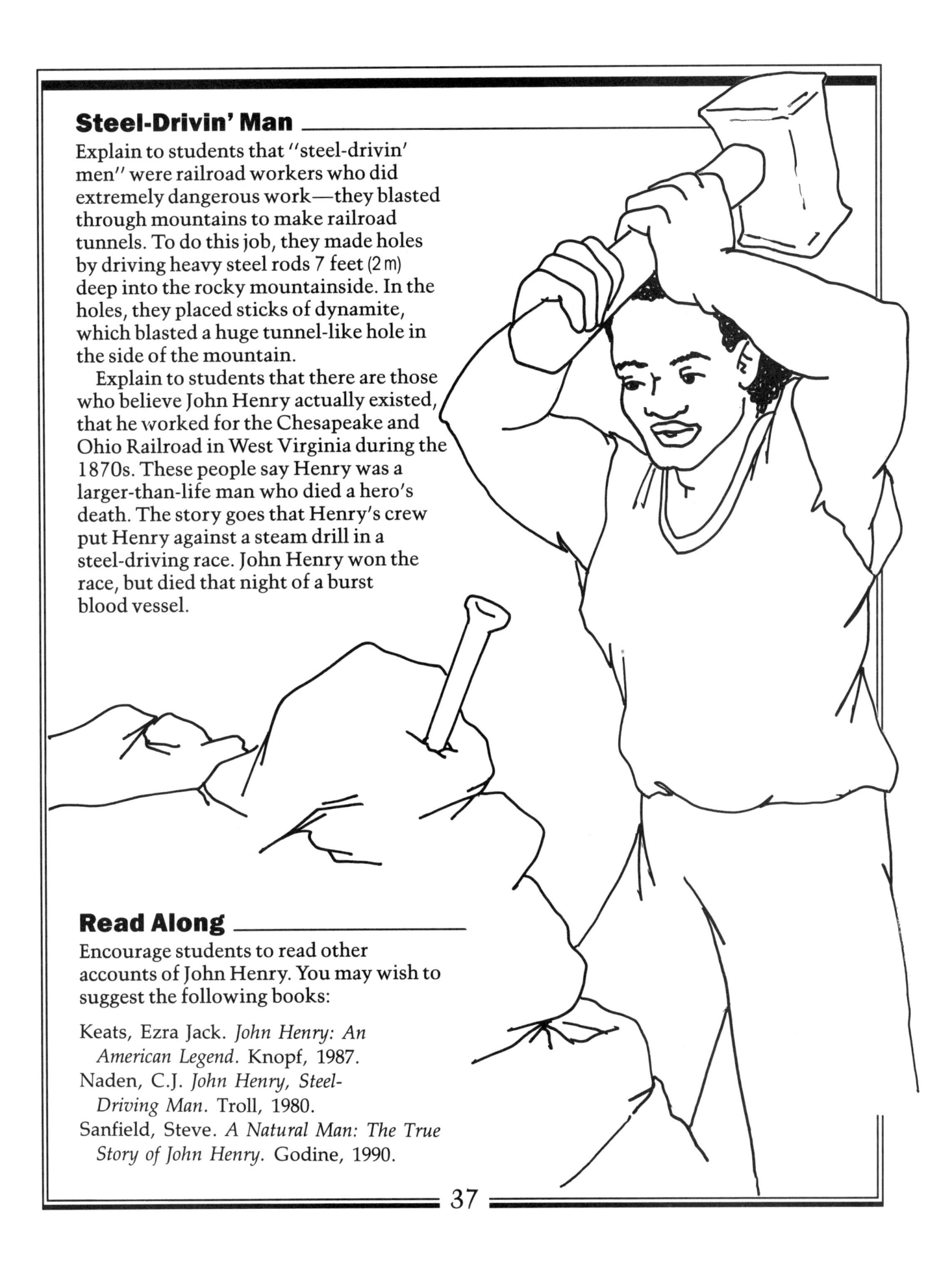

Explain to students that "steel-drivin' men" were railroad workers who did extremely dangerous work—they blasted through mountains to make railroad tunnels. To do this job, they made holes by driving heavy steel rods 7 feet (2 m) deep into the rocky mountainside. In the holes, they placed sticks of dynamite, which blasted a huge tunnel-like hole in the side of the mountain.

Explain to students that there are those who believe John Henry actually existed, that he worked for the Chesapeake and Ohio Railroad in West Virginia during the 1870s. These people say Henry was a larger-than-life man who died a hero's death. The story goes that Henry's crew put Henry against a steam drill in a steel-driving race. John Henry won the race, but died that night of a burst blood vessel.

Read Along

Encourage students to read other accounts of John Henry. You may wish to suggest the following books:

Keats, Ezra Jack. *John Henry: An American Legend.* Knopf, 1987.
Naden, C.J. *John Henry, Steel-Driving Man.* Troll, 1980.
Sanfield, Steve. *A Natural Man: The True Story of John Henry.* Godine, 1990.

Stormalong

On a globe or map, point out to students the New England seaports that were very busy in the 1700s due to the large number of cargo and passenger ships and boats that sailed in and out of port. Explain that sailors working the waters told stories of a daring and skillful fellow sailor whose name was Alfred Bulltop Stormalong, Old Stormalong, or Stormy for short.

Tell students that one tale suggests that while Stormalong and his crew were fishing one day, a giant squid wrapped fifty enormous legs around the boat's anchor. The squid's other fifty legs attached to the ocean floor. Old Stormy jumped overboard. The sea grew restless and then a great calm came over it. When the water settled, the boat began to rock . . . the anchor was free. Stormalong had tied every one of the squid's hundred legs into a sailor's knot.

Stormy Similes

Remind students that a simile is a phrase in which one thing is compared to another thing. Have students complete the following similes about Stormalong. Encourage them to use words that are related in some way to the region or environment from which the tale originated.

Ol' Stormy was as tall as _____

and as strong as _____.

Stormalong was as brave as _____.

Ol' Stormy could swim like _____.

Tell a Tall Tale

Have students write their own tall tale about Old Stormalong. Remind them that a tall tale is usually based on *some* bit of truth about the hero and often states some factual information about the region in which it was originally told. Point out that in the case of Stormalong, the region is New England.

Pecos Bill and Slue-Foot Sue

Share with students some information about Pecos Bill and his bride, Slue-Foot Sue. Ask students to tell if they think the story is true or a tall tale. Have them give at least two examples from the story to back up their conviction.

Tell students that Pecos Bill was a real cowboy who was raised by a coyote and taught by a grizzly bear. Pecos Bill invented the lasso, cattle branding, the cattle roundup, and the rodeo.

One day when Pecos Bill was standing on the banks of the Rio Grande, he saw a young woman, Slue-Foot Sue, riding a catfish the size of a whale. Pecos Bill fell head over heels in love with Sue, and they were married at once. Sue and Bill raised a large family, including a litter of coyote pups. People say the pups were so smart that two of them were elected to Congress!

Slue-Foot Sue

Ask a volunteer to define the word *slue*. Then have students, in groups of two or three, create tall tales to explain how Sue got the name *Slue-Foot*. Invite each group to dramatize its story for the class.

Folklore

Read aloud other stories about Pecos Bill and Slue-Foot Sue.

Blassingame, Wyatt. *Pecos Bill and the Wonderful Clothesline.* Garrard, 1978.
Dewey, Ariane. *Pecos Bill.* Greenwillow, 1983.
Lyman, Nanci A. *Pecos Bill.* Troll, 1980.
Stoutenberg, Adrien. *American Tall Tales.* Penguin, 1976.

Lasso

Remind students that Pecos Bill is believed to have been the person who invented the lasso. With a piece of rope or cord, demonstrate and then let students practice tying a lasso and other familiar knots.

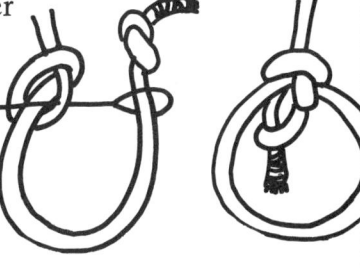

slipknot   square knot   lasso knot

Name _____   Date _____

Folk Heroes

Cut out the folk heroes at the bottom of the page. Glue the pictures on the map to show the region of the United States where each folk hero lived.

Paul Bunyan   Stormalong   John Henry   Pecos Bill

40

© 1992 by Troll Associates.

Name _____   Date _____

Caught in a Web

Label the web. Write the things John Henry and Paul Bunyan have in common in the center circles. Put the things that make them different in the circles at the sides.

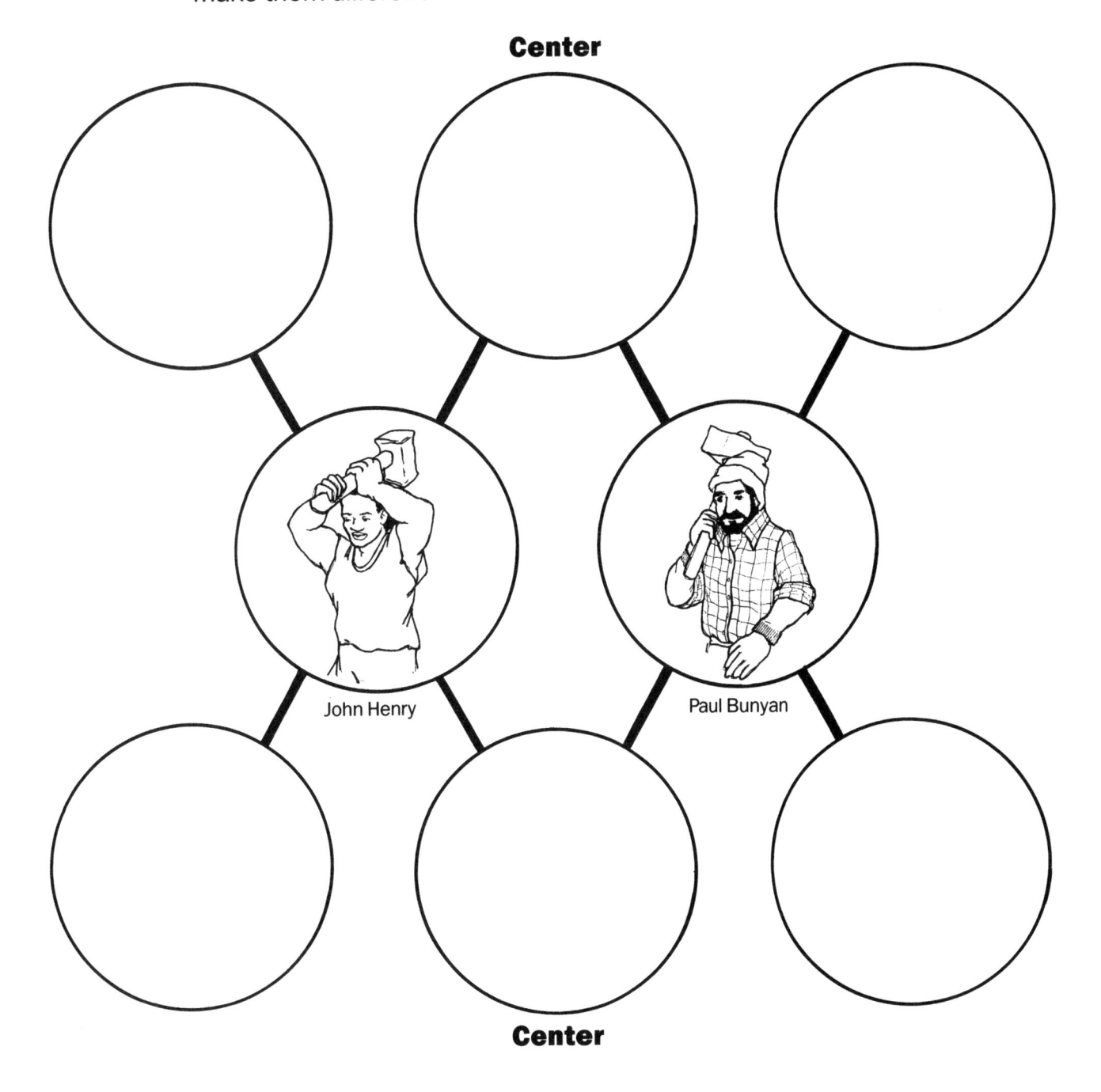

Center

John Henry

Paul Bunyan

Center

41

© 1992 by Troll Associates.

Generations/Heirlooms

The Keeping Quilt

Read *The Keeping Quilt* aloud to students. When you finish, ask them to explain the meaning of the title.

The Keeping Quilt by Patricia Polacco
(Simon & Schuster, 1988)

Family Traditions

Copy the following chart on the chalkboard. Have students compare the four generations of Patricia's family that are written about in *The Keeping Quilt*.

	Where they lived	What they wore to their wedding	What they added to their wedding bouquet	How they used the quilt
FIRST GENERATION				
SECOND GENERATION				
THIRD GENERATION				
FOURTH GENERATION				

My Family Roots

Have students research their family roots to find out in which country or countries their grandparents were born and the kind of clothing native to that country during that time period. Also, have students find out in which country or countries their parents were born and the kind of clothing that was popular when they were growing up. Last, have students record the country of their own birth. Encourage volunteers to share their information with the class.

The Patchwork Quilt

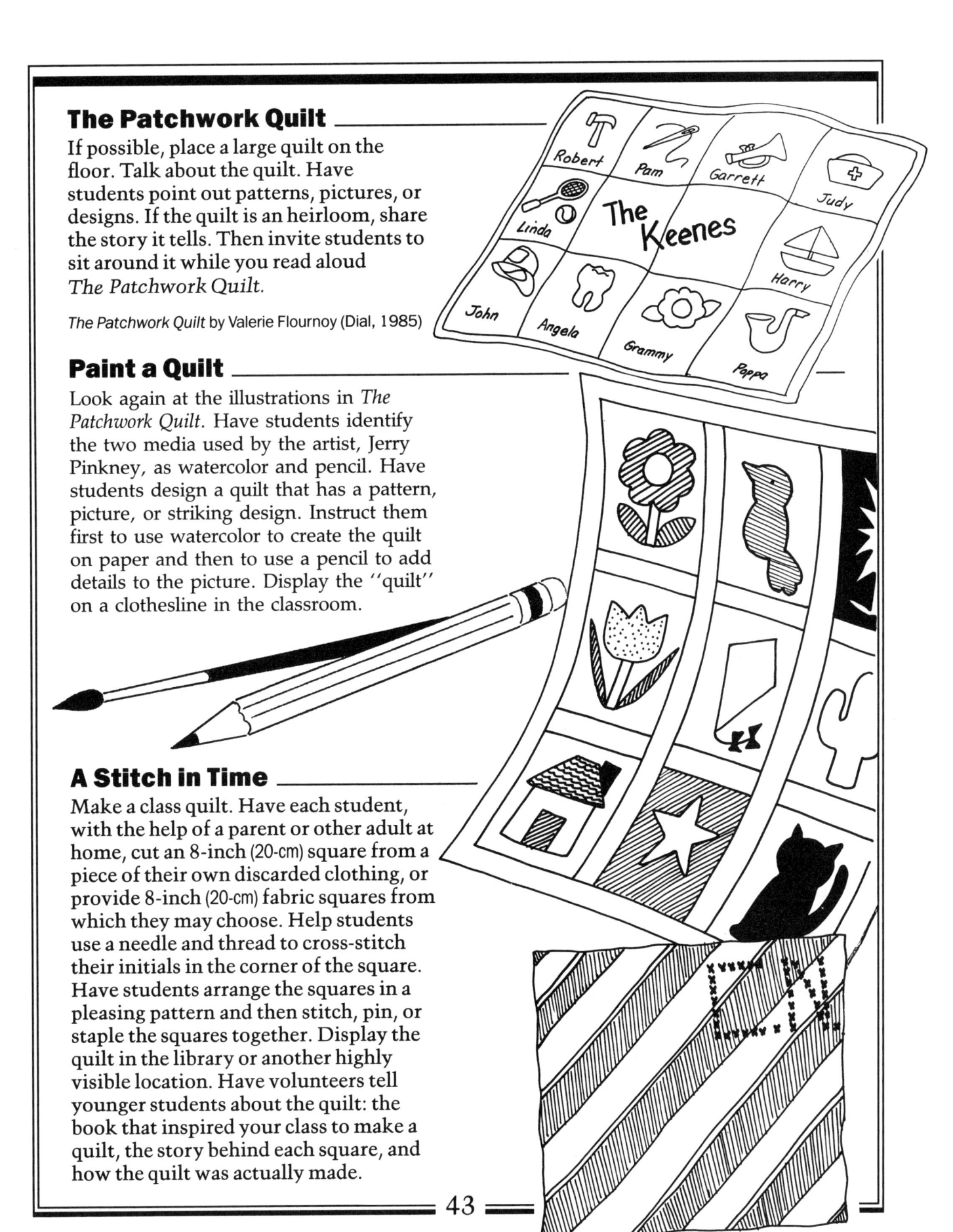

If possible, place a large quilt on the floor. Talk about the quilt. Have students point out patterns, pictures, or designs. If the quilt is an heirloom, share the story it tells. Then invite students to sit around it while you read aloud *The Patchwork Quilt*.

The Patchwork Quilt by Valerie Flournoy (Dial, 1985)

Paint a Quilt

Look again at the illustrations in *The Patchwork Quilt*. Have students identify the two media used by the artist, Jerry Pinkney, as watercolor and pencil. Have students design a quilt that has a pattern, picture, or striking design. Instruct them first to use watercolor to create the quilt on paper and then to use a pencil to add details to the picture. Display the "quilt" on a clothesline in the classroom.

A Stitch in Time

Make a class quilt. Have each student, with the help of a parent or other adult at home, cut an 8-inch (20-cm) square from a piece of their own discarded clothing, or provide 8-inch (20-cm) fabric squares from which they may choose. Help students use a needle and thread to cross-stitch their initials in the corner of the square. Have students arrange the squares in a pleasing pattern and then stitch, pin, or staple the squares together. Display the quilt in the library or another highly visible location. Have volunteers tell younger students about the quilt: the book that inspired your class to make a quilt, the story behind each square, and how the quilt was actually made.

Share an Heirloom

Invite interested students to share family heirlooms. They may wish to show pictures of and tell the stories behind the furniture, wedding dresses, antique cars, quilts, or other items that have been passed down from one generation to the next. When possible, students may wish to bring in smaller family treasures such as antique toys, hand-embroidered pillowcases, jewelry, and the like.

Stories to Grow On

Have students interview older family members to gather information and favorite stories. Tell students to add to these interviews humorous, interesting, or otherwise noteworthy stories and information about themselves. Encourage students to share their stories with the youngest members of their families so that traditions, events, and other family stories will not be forgotten. Point out that keeping a family scrapbook or creating a family newsletter is another way to hand down family traditions.

Through Grandpa's Eyes

Have students close their eyes (or darken the room) and listen to identify sounds in or near the classroom, such as a clock ticking, a car passing, or water running.

Show the cover of *Through Grandpa's Eyes*. Point out Grandpa and John. Explain that although John's Grandpa is blind, he has his own way of "seeing" things. Invite students to listen as you read the story aloud to find out how John learns to "see through his Grandpa's eyes." After reading the story, have students discuss ways Grandpa uses his other senses to "see" the world.

Through Grandpa's Eyes by Patricia MacLachlan (Harper, 1980)

Grandpa's Legacy

Have students list at least eight adjectives that describe Grandpa. Some adjectives might include *perceptive*, *observant*, *gentle*, *witty*, and *loving*. From the lists, have students discuss the legacy that Grandpa will leave John and the generations that follow. Point out that legacies and heirlooms do not have to be *objects*; often they are valuable qualities such as a sense of humor, a set of values or traditions, or an artistic ability.

Use Grandpa's Eyes

Blindfold volunteers and have them use some of Grandpa's "tricks" to see things.
1. Fill a cup with water.
2. Play a musical instrument.
3. Mold a clay bird.
4. Dry a dish.
5. Go outdoors and identify the direction in which the wind is blowing.

Name _____   Date _____

The Way Things Were

Ask your grandparents, parents, aunts and uncles, or older brothers and sisters the questions on this page to find out how things were the same or different when they were younger.

1. SCHOOL

How were schools the same as or different from the way they are now?

_____
_____
_____

2. RECREATION

What did you do for fun? In what way was this activity the same as or different from what people do now?

_____
_____
_____

3. CLOTHING

How was the clothing you wore the same as or different from the clothing people wear now?

_____
_____
_____

4. PRICES

How much did you pay for certain things then compared to now? For example, how much did a newspaper cost? What was the price of milk and bread?

_____
_____
_____

© 1992 by Troll Associates.

Name _____ Date _____

Family Tree

Write the necessary information in each apple to complete your family tree.

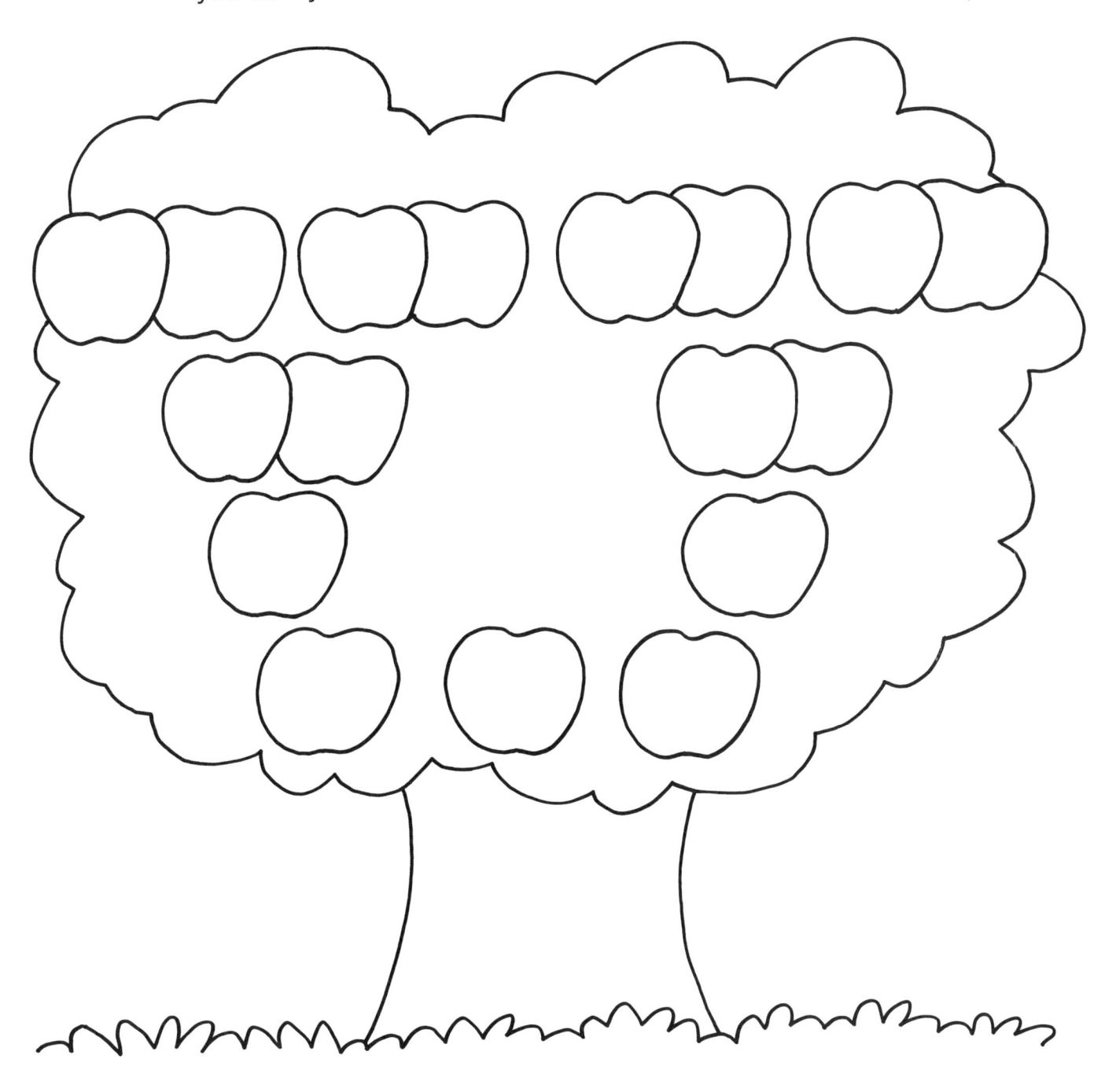

The Human Body

Skeleton

Display a picture of a human skeleton or, if possible, a model of one. Have students look at the skeleton and then guess the total number of bones that create the complex structure. See who can come the closest to the correct answer of 206.

The Long and Short of It

Point to your femur (thigh bone) and measure it, if possible. Tell students that the femur in a 6-foot-tall (1.8-m-tall) man would be about 20 inches (50 cm) long, making it the longest bone in the body. Explain that the stirrup (in the inner ear), the smallest bone in the body, is only about one tenth of an inch (one fourth of a cm) long.

Have students draw the femur and stirrup to scale and label them.

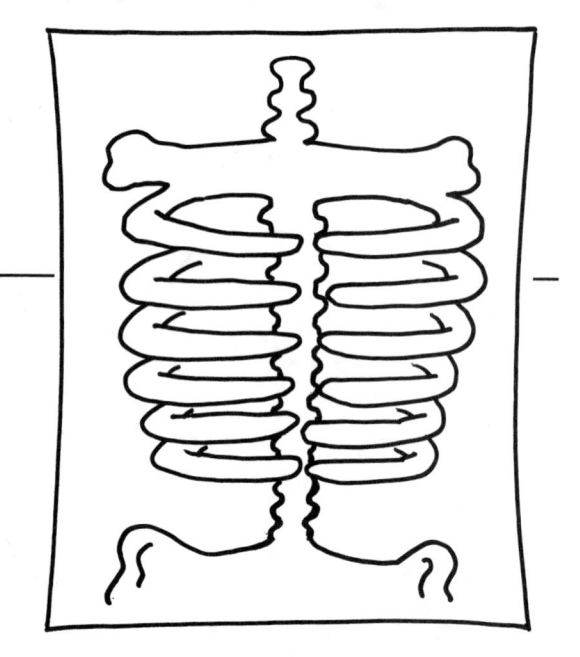

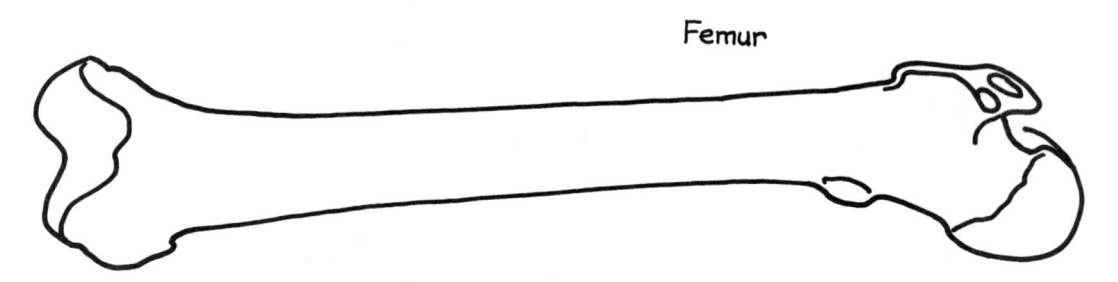

Femur

Stirrup

Spine

Remind students that the thirty-three bones, or vertebrae, in the backbone, or spine, are the most important bones in the body because they make it possible for humans to stand upright, to bend, and to move easily.

Have students work in pairs. Ask one student to demonstrate movements in which he or she uses his or her backbone: stretching, bending at the waist, twisting the trunk, and so forth. Have the other student place his or her hands on the partner's back to feel the vertebrae move.

Ask students to speculate on what would happen if humans did not have backbones.

Body Facts

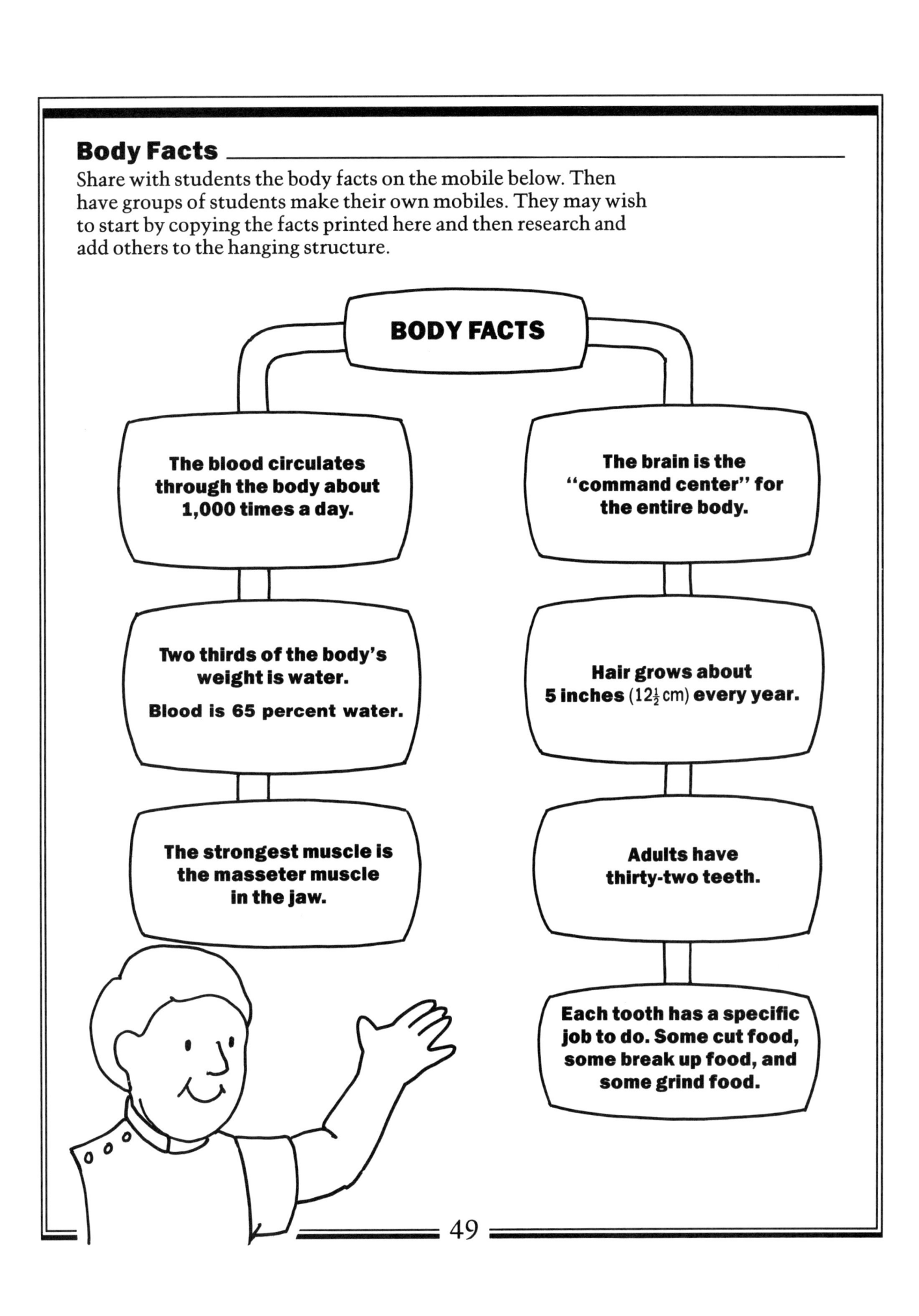

Share with students the body facts on the mobile below. Then have groups of students make their own mobiles. They may wish to start by copying the facts printed here and then research and add others to the hanging structure.

BODY FACTS

- The blood circulates through the body about 1,000 times a day.
- Two thirds of the body's weight is water. Blood is 65 percent water.
- The strongest muscle is the masseter muscle in the jaw.

- The brain is the "command center" for the entire body.
- Hair grows about 5 inches (12½ cm) every year.
- Adults have thirty-two teeth.
- Each tooth has a specific job to do. Some cut food, some break up food, and some grind food.

First Aid

Inform students that most accidents occur in and around the home and that knowing what to do for an injured person might save his or her life. Consult a first-aid reference book and then demonstrate each of the following first-aid techniques for students. Then have students practice them on partners. Check to be sure students can administer them properly.

MILD BURN
Soak in ice water. Then apply a dry dressing.

FAINTING
If person is dizzy, help him or her to lower the head between the knees. Loosen clothing and open windows.

BEE STING
If possible, remove stinger. Apply solution of ammonia and water or damp baking soda. Call doctor, if necessary.

MINOR CUT
Wash with soap and water. Apply antiseptic and cover with bandage.

First-Aid Book

Have students write and illustrate their own books showing each of the first-aid techniques demonstrated above.

First-Aid Kit

Have students gather the materials to make a classroom first-aid kit. You should include the following items: sterile gauze pads and bandages, aspirin, hydrogen peroxide, antibiotic cream, cotton balls, adhesive tape, thermometer, tweezers, elastic bandages, scissors, safety pins, antiseptic spray.

Medical Milestones

Copy the following medical milestones on index cards. Assign each card to a student or group of students. Have them find out the year in which the event occurred and print it clearly at the top of the card. Have students present their milestones to the class. Then help students make a time line using the cards.

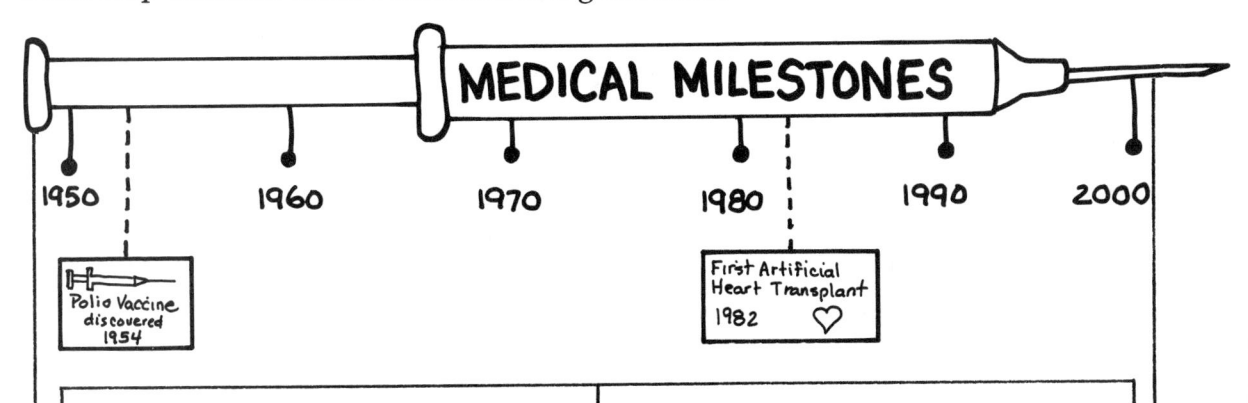

The first CAT scan is used to take clear pictures of cross sections of the body, especially the brain. (1972)	First lifesaving surgery is performed on a baby while it is still inside its mother. (1990)
The first artificial heart is implanted in a human. (1982)	X-rays are first used. (1895)
Penicillin is discovered. (1928)	Polio vaccine is discovered. (1954)
Aspirin is found to be effective against strokes. (1990)	

A Doctor Directory

Have students work together to make a directory of doctors. Include the following specialists and a brief description of their expertise: allergist, anesthesiologist, cardiologist, dermatologist, gastroenterologist, gerontologist, gynecologist, hematologist, immunologist, neurologist, obstetrician, ophthalmologist, orthopedist, orthodontist, pathologist, pediatrician, plastic surgeon, psychiatrist, radiologist, rheumatologist, and urologist.

Name _____   Date _____

Southpaws

A southpaw is a left-handed person. Many very famous and gifted people throughout history were southpaws. Leonardo da Vinci and Michelangelo, two of the greatest sculptors of all time, were both left-handed. Maybe *you* are a southpaw, or perhaps you know someone who is. Take a survey. Find out how many left-handed people you know.

Interview twenty people to find out if they are right-handed or left-handed. Have them write their initials inside the graph to show the results.

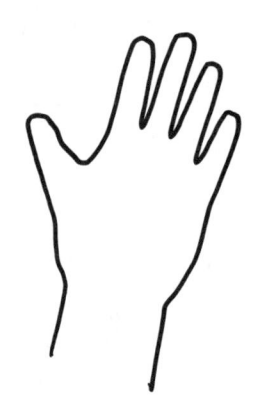

Number of Right-Handed Friends

Number of Left-Handed Friends

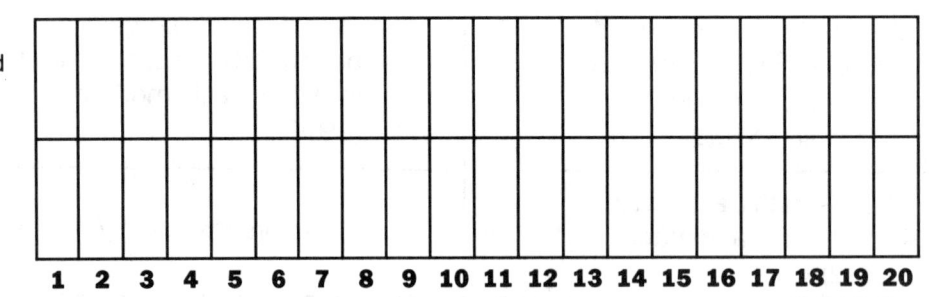

1 2 3 4 5 6 7 8 9 10 11 12 13 14 15 16 17 18 19 20

Scientists say that about one in every twenty people in the world is left-handed. Did you find the same results?

Ask your left-handed friends if they have had to make adjustments to live in a right-handed world. Have them describe the adjustments. Some situations requiring adjustments might include: opening doors with knobs on the right side, playing baseball, eating beside someone who is right-handed, or playing a musical instrument.

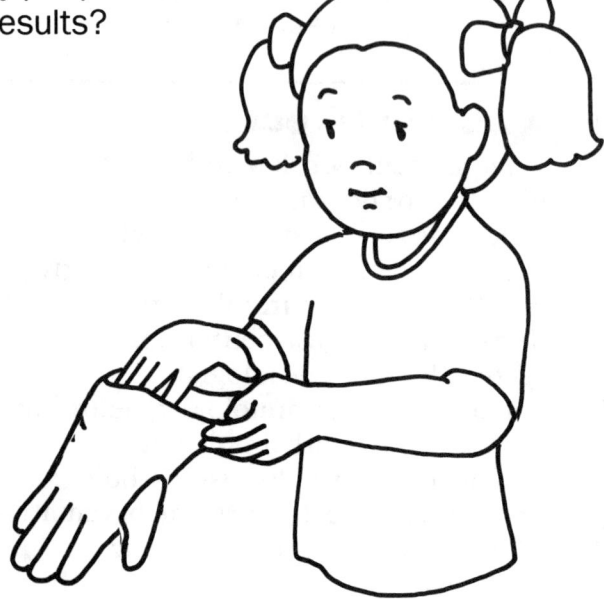

52

© 1992 by Troll Associates.

Name _____   Date _____

Fingerprints

In movies, TV shows, books, and plays, the "bad guys" often leave fingerprints on something and are later caught because of them. A fingerprint is considered *proof* of someone's identity. That is because no two people have the same markings on their fingertips.

See for yourself. Press each of your fingers on a black ink pad and then in the spaces provided. Compare your fingerprints to the prints made by your friends. Can you identify your own? How?

Left Hand		
Ring	Middle	Index
Pinkie	Thumb	

Right Hand		
Index	Middle	Ring
Thumb		Pinkie

53

© 1992 by Troll Associates.

Inventions

Who Were the First People to Fly?

Tell students that in 1783 a French doctor named Jean François Pilâtre de Rozier invented a balloon that took him flying high into the air. Explain that balloons were easy to fly, but that they could not be steered very well. As a result, many people worked to make a flying machine that could be steered with accuracy.

Tell students that in 1903 two brothers created and then flew an airplane powered by an engine, in Kitty Hawk, North Carolina. On their first flight, Wilbur and Orville Wright kept their plane in the air for about twelve seconds and went almost 120 feet (14.5 m). By their fourth flight, the brothers flew 852 feet (21.3 m) in about a minute.

Have students find out which of the Wright brothers, Orville or Wilbur, was the person who actually flew the first plane. Have them find out how the brothers decided who would fly first.

History of Aviation

Have students write a letter to the Experimental Aircraft Association requesting information about airplanes and the history of aviation. Use the information you receive to make an aviation bulletin board.

Experimental Aircraft Association
Whittman Airfield
Oshkosh, WI 54903

Future Aircraft

Remind students that today we have great supersonic jets that can fly for hours without refueling. Display pictures of new aircrafts and discuss their features.

Invite students to invent a flying craft of their own. They may make three-dimensional models of the craft or draw diagrams on paper. Have them name the craft, describe its features, and tell where they intend to fly it.

Thomas Edison

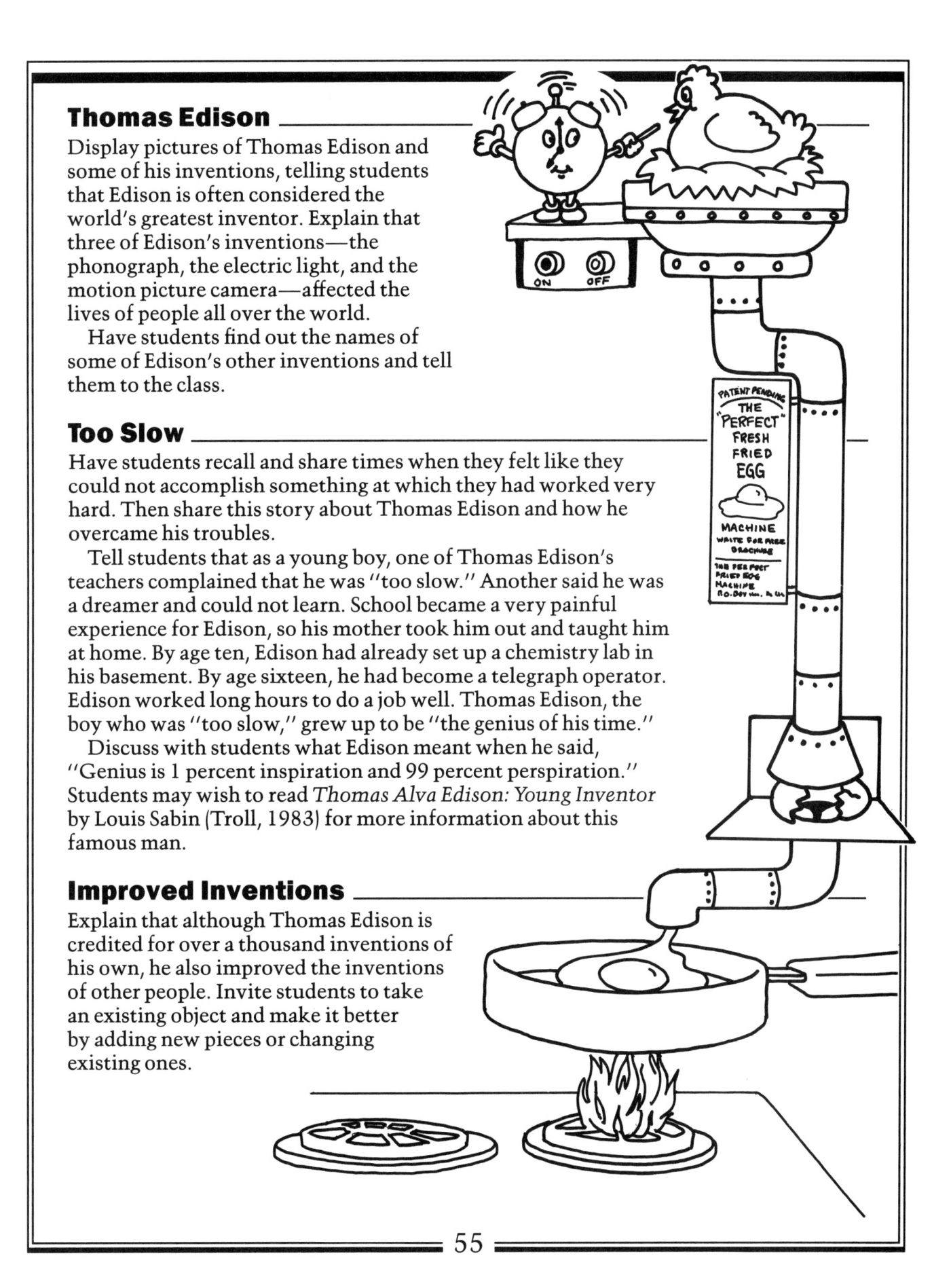

Display pictures of Thomas Edison and some of his inventions, telling students that Edison is often considered the world's greatest inventor. Explain that three of Edison's inventions—the phonograph, the electric light, and the motion picture camera—affected the lives of people all over the world.

Have students find out the names of some of Edison's other inventions and tell them to the class.

Too Slow

Have students recall and share times when they felt like they could not accomplish something at which they had worked very hard. Then share this story about Thomas Edison and how he overcame his troubles.

Tell students that as a young boy, one of Thomas Edison's teachers complained that he was "too slow." Another said he was a dreamer and could not learn. School became a very painful experience for Edison, so his mother took him out and taught him at home. By age ten, Edison had already set up a chemistry lab in his basement. By age sixteen, he had become a telegraph operator. Edison worked long hours to do a job well. Thomas Edison, the boy who was "too slow," grew up to be "the genius of his time."

Discuss with students what Edison meant when he said, "Genius is 1 percent inspiration and 99 percent perspiration." Students may wish to read *Thomas Alva Edison: Young Inventor* by Louis Sabin (Troll, 1983) for more information about this famous man.

Improved Inventions

Explain that although Thomas Edison is credited for over a thousand inventions of his own, he also improved the inventions of other people. Invite students to take an existing object and make it better by adding new pieces or changing existing ones.

Alexander Graham Bell

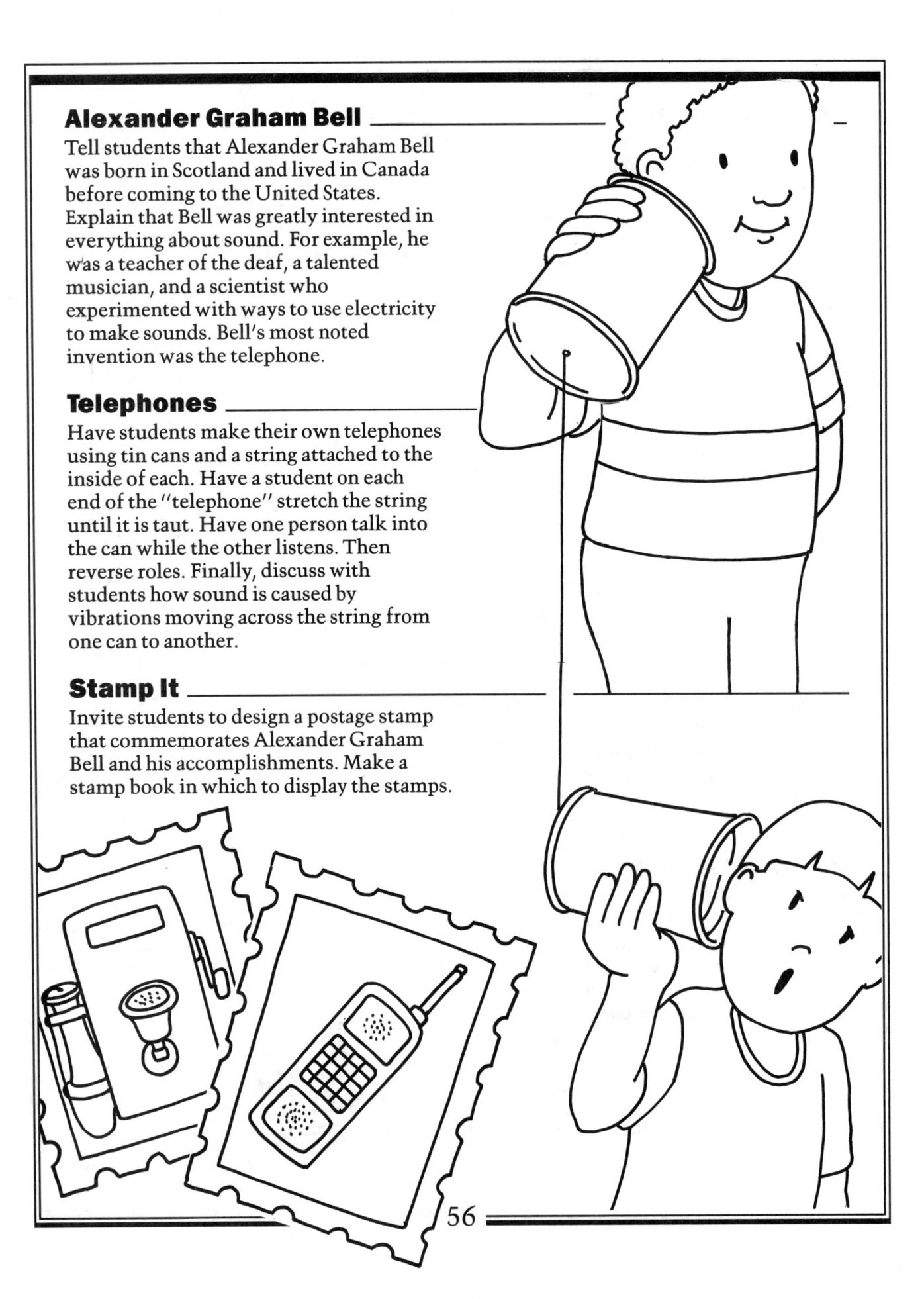

Tell students that Alexander Graham Bell was born in Scotland and lived in Canada before coming to the United States. Explain that Bell was greatly interested in everything about sound. For example, he was a teacher of the deaf, a talented musician, and a scientist who experimented with ways to use electricity to make sounds. Bell's most noted invention was the telephone.

Telephones

Have students make their own telephones using tin cans and a string attached to the inside of each. Have a student on each end of the "telephone" stretch the string until it is taut. Have one person talk into the can while the other listens. Then reverse roles. Finally, discuss with students how sound is caused by vibrations moving across the string from one can to another.

Stamp It

Invite students to design a postage stamp that commemorates Alexander Graham Bell and his accomplishments. Make a stamp book in which to display the stamps.

Who Invented Basketball?

Explain to students that basketball is called "the international game," largely because it is played by people in nearly every country in the world. The sport, which is so popular today, was invented by James A. Naismith more than one hundred years ago.

Have students work in pairs to research the game of basketball. Tell them to find out on which two games basketball is based and how the game got its name. Encourage students to discover other interesting facts about basketball.

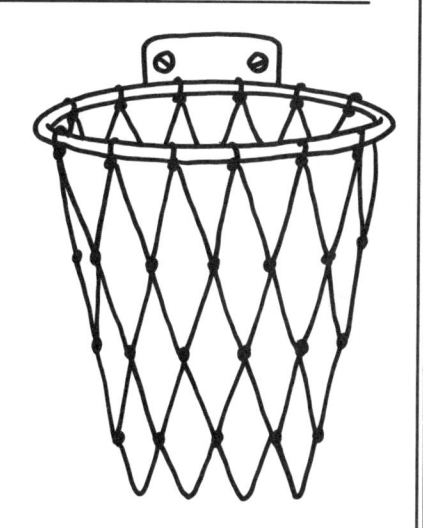

Combined Sports

Have students work in small groups to invent a new sport. Encourage them to combine the best parts of two well-known sports to create their new sport. Tell each group to name their game, write the rules, list the equipment needed to play, and then practice playing it. When they are ready, have students demonstrate their games to the class.

Zany Inventions for Pets

Bulletproof Vests for Dogs

Tell students that because many dogs are accidentally shot and killed each year, a Belgian firm invented a bulletproof vest for dogs. The vest, used primarily by police dogs, is similar in design to the ones worn by police officers.

Dog Eyeglasses

Tell students that in 1975, a French ophthalmologist, Denise Lemière, invented glasses with prescription lenses to correct her dog's failing eyesight.

Car Seats for Cats

Safety councils across the world have discovered that adults who wear seat belts and children who are strapped in car seats have far fewer injuries than those who do not use the safety devices. So why not a car seat designed for a pet? Paul Rux introduced the first pet car seat in 1983.

Pet Peeves

Read this saying to students: *Necessity is the mother of invention.* Ask students to explain what it means.

Then have students brainstorm problems they have with their pets for which they have no solutions. Challenge them to invent solutions for their "pet peeves."

Answers to Activity Sheet: **1.** Louis Pasteur **2.** Samuel Morse **3.** Adolphe Sax **4.** Rudolf Diesel **5.** Gabriel Fahrenheit

Name _____ Date _____

Name the Inventor

Many inventions are named after the people who developed them. For each invention below, write the name of the inventor. Use an encyclopedia or other reference source to help you.

1. the pasteurization process
   _____

2. the system of communication using dots and dashes
   _____

3. the saxophone
   _____

4. the diesel engine
   _____

5. the Fahrenheit thermometer
   _____

If you could have any invention named after you, what invention would it be and why? Write your answers on the lines below.

_____
_____
_____
_____
_____
_____

© 1992 by Troll Associates.

Mysteries

Crime Doesn't Pay

Ask students to explain what a mystery is. Point out that a mystery is a form of writing with special characteristics that set it apart from other forms of writing. Explain that to be considered a true mystery, a story must include a crime, a criminal, a detective, and clues. In addition, something must remain undisclosed until the conclusion of the story. Point out that literary techniques called suspense and foreshadowing are often present in a mystery and define the terms. Then explain to students that the purpose of these techniques is to capture the reader's curiosity until the very end of the story. Encourage students to share their favorite mysteries.

To Catch a Thief

Tell students that many different kinds of crimes can be included in a mystery, such as murder, kidnapping, or theft. Have students brainstorm the kinds of crimes they might find in a mystery story. Encourage students to think about mystery stories they have read or seen on television to help them with their responses.

Whodunit?

Explain to students that the characters in a mystery must be interesting as well as believable. Point out that the criminal must appear early in the story, but that his or her identity is not usually revealed until the end of the story. Part of the fun of reading a mystery is trying to figure out "whodunit." Explain that in some mysteries, the criminal is often someone you would least expect to be guilty. Now ask students to pretend they are mystery writers and look at these pictures of four convicted criminals. Have students decide what kind of crime might have been committed by each criminal and explain why.

Mystery Writers

Sir Arthur Conan Doyle

Tell students that Sir Arthur Conan Doyle was born in England on May 22, 1859. He started writing to supplement his income as a ship's doctor on long ocean voyages.

Explain that as a young child, Doyle read so much that when he was ten his local library told his mother that books would not be checked out for her son more than two times a day! Tell students that Doyle once wrote and illustrated a book about a man and a tiger, but merged the two characters into one in only a few pages. He once told his mother that it was easy to get people into scrapes, but not so easy to get them out! Point out to students that many mystery writers face that same problem.

Have students create a seemingly impossible situation with a character of their choice and then trade with a classmate to see what solutions he or she can devise.

E. L. Konigsburg

Tell students that writer and illustrator E. L. Konigsburg claims that a kindergartner lives inside her, telling her that books should be both shown *and* told! Her interest in art has flavored several of her books, such as the Newbery Medal–winning *From the Mixed-Up Files of Mrs. Basil E. Frankweiler* (New York: Atheneum, 1970).

Explain to students that Konigsburg's advice to aspiring young writers is "Don't talk about doing it—*do it!*" Have students make a list of rules for good writing habits and post them on a bulletin board for future reference.

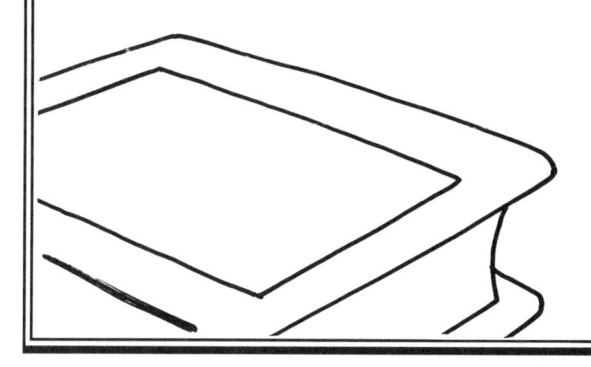

Monster Mysteries

Loch Ness Monster
Display a picture of Loch Ness in Scotland and tell students that a mysterious creature called the Loch Ness monster is said to live beneath the coffee-colored water. Tell students that peat in the water causes its dark color. Explain that the water is so murky that divers cannot see more than 12 inches (30 cm) in front of them. Explain that thousands of people claim to have seen the monster, but no proof of its existence has been found.

Have students make a diorama of Loch Ness, adding peat (or soil) to water in a fish tank or other container. Use rocks to create the rocky shoreline.

Say "Cheese!"
Tell students that many people have tried to photograph Nessie, as the monster is often called. Display several books on the Loch Ness monster and have students discuss the photographs. Ask students to examine each one carefully and note any common characteristics. Point out that the photographs are too hazy to be proof of the monster's existence, but that it seems fair to think there may be some sort of large creature in Loch Ness. Divide the class into two teams to debate the existence of the Loch Ness monster based on the photographs. Have students on each team prepare a case for its viewpoint and support it with photographs from the books and with clay models that show what the team thinks Nessie looks like. Give each team several minutes to present its viewpoint, and then one minute per team for a rebuttal. When the debate is over, have students put their clay models in the diorama from the previous activity.

Will the Real Monster Please Stand Up?
Tell students that in the early 1960s, the Loch Ness Phenomena Investigation Bureau was set up to collect eyewitness accounts from people who claimed to have seen the Loch Ness monster. The bureau also tried to get more accurate photographs. By 1967, they were filming and photographing over 70 percent of the lake from May to October, when most sightings reportedly occurred. All reported sightings were carefully analyzed, and forms were designed to record all important information.

Have students brainstorm the kinds of information the bureau might have requested on a sighting report and design the form. Then have some students pretend they saw the monster while other students interview them and record their responses on their forms.

More Monster Mysteries

Bigfoot Makes News!

Tell students that a giant, hairy, humanlike creature called Bigfoot is said to roam the forests of the United States and British Columbia. Sightings have been reported, photographs have been taken, film has been shot, and models of giant footprints in forests have been cast that seem to lend evidence to this creature's existence. Explain to students that like the Loch Ness monster, the true existence of Bigfoot has not yet been confirmed—and for similar reasons. The photographs are unclear, the film is too blurry, and the footprints could have been made as a joke. Disbelievers claim that Bigfoot is really a giant ape or bear, or even a human being in a costume. Point out, however, that a film of Bigfoot taken by one man was analyzed by expert filmmakers at Walt Disney Studios. They decided that the film was not a hoax.

Display books containing photographs of Bigfoot and discuss its appearance. Elicit the features common to most photographs—very tall, heavy, hairy, walks upright, and has a pointed head. Now ask half the students to act as newspaper reporters and make a list of interview questions they would like to ask Bigfoot, while the other half of the class responds as Bigfoot. Have students tape-record their interviews.

Let's Make Tracks

Explain to students that although many of Bigfoot's footprints have been found, none has been recognized as proof of Bigfoot's existence. Tell students that studies of the footprints have shown them to be between 1–2 feet (30–60 cm) long! Some footprints show a toe that is much larger than the others.

Pour some talcum powder or flour into a shallow tray. Ask each student to remove one shoe and sock, step firmly into the powder, and then step onto a sheet of black construction paper to make a print. Have several students stand by to help steady the students making the prints. Then display photographs of Bigfoot's footprints. Have students measure their own footprints and then compare them with Bigfoot's.

Name _____ Date _____

Clues and More Clues

Read *From the Mixed-up Files of Mrs. Basil E. Frankweiler* and think about its characters. How does Konigsburg describe Claudia? What techniques does the author use in her description?

_____
_____
_____

A good mystery writer gives the reader clues to solve the mystery. Look back through the book and jot down a few page numbers that mark the places where you first began to suspect that Angel had been carved by Michelangelo. Keep a record of each clue you find.

Clue #1: _____

Clue #2: _____

Clue #3: _____

Now go back and discuss which clues actually lead to solving the mystery.

Pretend that several pages important to the story were missing from your book. Make up two clues that could be added to the story that would *not* change the outcome but that would add to the excitement.

New Clue #1: _____
_____

New Clue #2: _____
_____

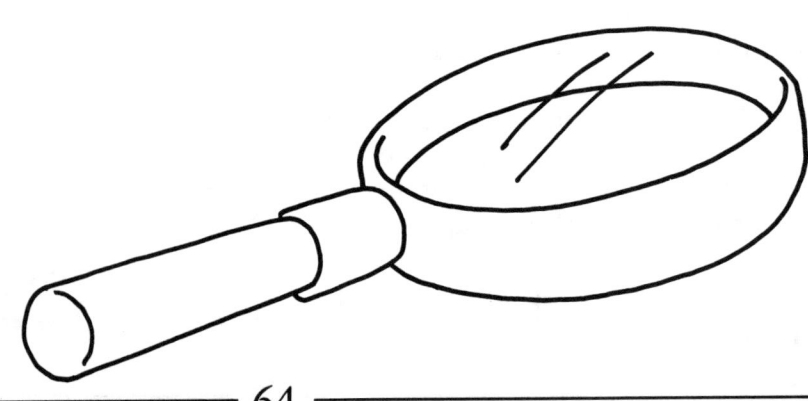

© 1992 by Troll Associates.

Name _____   Date _____

Rules for a Mystery

Good writing is more than putting pencil to paper. A good motto to follow is, "Think before you write." Toss your ideas around in your mind so you know what you're going to write about. This is especially important in mystery writing. Good mystery writers usually know what's going to happen to each character in each situation before they begin writing.

Now study these rules for a mystery—they will help you make sure your ideas make sense, follow a logical order, and are interesting.

MYSTERY RULEBOOK

1. There must be a crime.
2. The criminal must appear early in the story, but his or her identity is kept secret.
3. All clues must be made available to the reader.
4. The detective must try to catch the criminal, and the criminal must try to get away.

Now it's time for you to try your hand at writing your own mystery. First, complete the charts below to set up the framework of your story, then write your rough draft on another sheet of paper. Remember to think before you write!

Criminal

Name: _____

Description: _____
_____

Crime

Who: _____

What: _____

Where: _____

When: _____

Why: _____

Detective

Name: _____

Description: _____
_____

Clues

1. _____
2. _____
3. _____
4. _____
5. _____

© 1992 by Troll Associates.

The Ocean

Deep-Sea "Monsters"

Invite students to take an imaginary journey with you to the bottom of the ocean. Darken the room. Have students imagine they are in a deep-sea vessel that is going under the water.

Tell them that they are passing through the top layer of the ocean, the part that is moved by the tides. Have them "look" for starfish, sand dollars, crabs, and clams.

Explain that the imaginary sea vessel is diving deeper. Have students look out the window and watch the interesting underwater scenery passing by. Invite students to "look" at the large sea animals swimming in the middle depths of the ocean: sailfish, tuna, octopus, squid, whales, walrus, and sea lions.

Continue the imaginary voyage by having students pretend that their vessel has settled on the ocean floor. Tell them that this is a zone of complete darkness and that there are many odd-looking fish living here. Explain that these deep-water fish are slow swimmers and that to make up for lack of speed, many of them have enormous mouths with long, sharp teeth to help them get food. Have students "look" for the big-mouthed fish. Then have them "look" at some other luminous "sea monsters"—fish that have lights on their bodies or lights on antennae that extend from their faces.

Spooky Fish

Have students draw pictures of the fish they imagine would be on the bottom of the ocean. Then display pictures of real deep-sea "monsters." Invite students to label the pictures for an ocean pictionary.

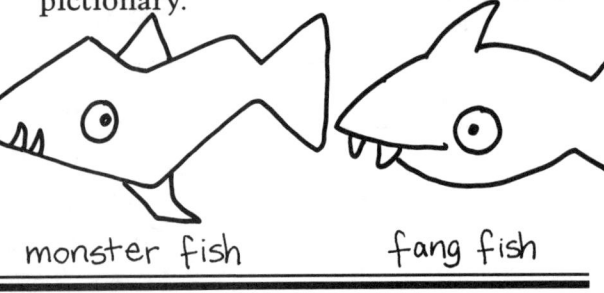

monster fish   fang fish   howling fish   smirking fish

Ocean Mammals

Remind students that whales, dolphins, porpoises, and manatees are mammals. Tell them that such animals are distant relatives of sea creatures that once lived on land but that for some unknown reason, returned to the sea millions of years ago. Tell students that the flippers on ocean mammals were once forelegs and that their back legs disappeared altogether.

Explain that although whales, dolphins, porpoises, and manatees look like and swim like fish, there are several distinct differences between these animals and fish.

- Mammals do not have gills; they breathe air.
- Mammals do not lay eggs; they bear their young alive.
- Baby sea mammals do not eat plants or fish; their mothers nurse them.
- Unlike fish, mammals are warm-blooded. They have layers of fat to keep them from losing too much body heat in cold waters.

Porpoise Poems

Have students follow the pattern for writing *diamante*, a type of poetry shaped like a diamond. Encourage them to use one of the ocean mammals as the topic for their poem.

Line 1: [the topic] a noun
Line 2: two adjectives
Line 3: three verbs
Line 4: four nouns
Line 5: three verbs
Line 6: two adjectives
Line 7: [same as line 1]

Classification Chart

Have students collect pictures of marine animals. Have them classify the animals as mammals or fish. In addition to the four animals discussed above, there are many other ocean mammals, including seals, otters, sea lions, and walrus.

Ocean Plants

Ask students to name kinds of ocean plants they know about. The lists may include kinds of seaweed and sargassum (sar-GAS-sum). Draw the following diagram on the chalkboard and lead a discussion about how ocean plants and land plants differ. Note particularly the absence of flowers, fruits, roots, and stems on ocean plants.

Seaweed

Harvesting the Sea

Tell students that many people in the world, especially the Japanese, harvest large amounts of seaweed for food. If possible, provide a large piece of sea kelp. Have students put the kelp out to dry. When the kelp is dry, invite students to taste it. Have students make a list of other edible food sources from the sea.

The Ocean Floor

Tell students that if the water in the ocean could be drained, a fantastic landscape would be revealed. Canyons deeper than the Grand Canyon and mountains higher than the Rocky Mountains would be uncovered. Point out that many islands are really peaks of submerged mountains. Have students locate the "peaks" of Hawaii, Bermuda, and Puerto Rico on a map or globe. Encourage them to find other submerged mountains.

Have students define these words that describe the ocean floor: *basin*, *trench*, *ridge*, and *rise*. Help them find examples of each landform on a relief globe.

Relief Map

Invite pairs of students to make a relief map of the ocean floor. Mix and knead the following ingredients to make relief clay:

- 2 cups (500 ml) self-rising flour
- 2 tablespoons (30 ml) salt
- 1 cup (250 ml) boiling water
- 2 tablespoons (30 ml) alum
- 2 tablespoons (30 ml) cooking oil
- food coloring

Divide clay into three piles. Add a few drops of brown, green, or blue food coloring to each pile and mix.

Each student will need a piece of cardboard on which to build the relief map. Instruct them to mold the clay to form basins, trenches, ridges, and rises on the ocean floor. Students may wish to add plants, rocks, shells, and the like to complete their map of the ocean floor.

Treasure Seekers

Tell students that the sea is a graveyard for wrecked ships and that divers seek out the shipwrecks in search of treasures such as silver and gold.

Invite interested students to find out about underwater explorers, sunken ships, and treasures of the sea. You might suggest that they research and report on one or more of the following topics:

Jacques-Yves Cousteau, famous underwater explorer

Titanic, ship thought to be "unsinkable"

Trieste, a bell-shaped diving vessel for deep-sea exploration

Andrea Doria, sunken Italian ocean liner

Atlantis, legendary island that sank into the Atlantic Ocean

Mel Fisher, treasure hunter

Underwater Stations

Explain that oceanographers are beginning to find ways to use the ocean's wealth as a source of food and energy, and that some scientists are already planning underwater stations in which people will work and live. Have students draw and label diagrams of their own futuristic underwater stations.

Record Breakers

Draw and cut out seven large fish. Post the fish on a bulletin board or use them as a border around a doorway. Print one superlative on each fish. Have students find and record the marine animal that holds each record.

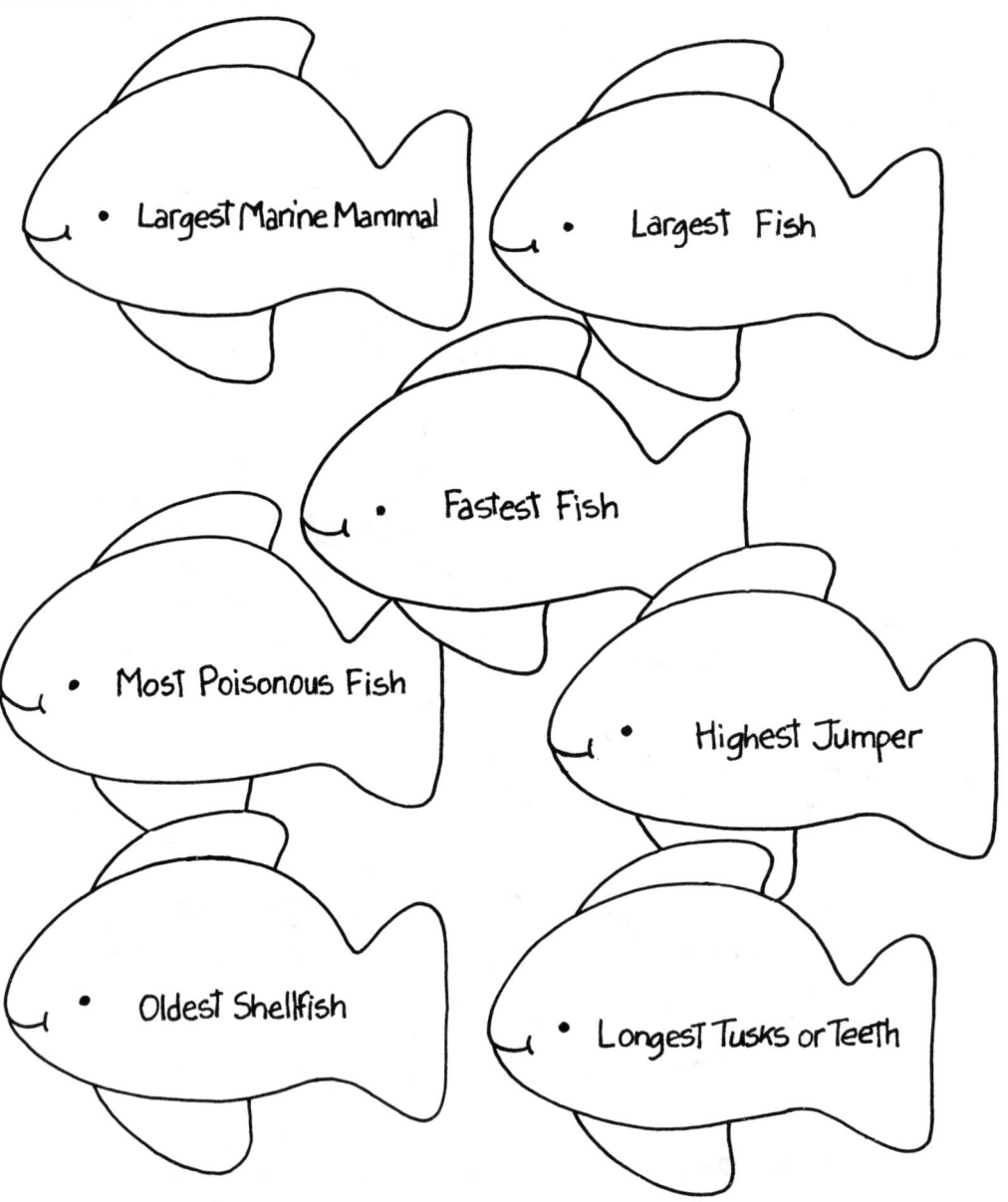

- Largest Marine Mammal
- Largest Fish
- Fastest Fish
- Most Poisonous Fish
- Highest Jumper
- Oldest Shellfish
- Longest Tusks or Teeth

Fastest Sea Animals

Tell students that champion swimmers can swim about 5 miles (8 km) per hour. In contrast, the sailfish can swim up to 70 miles (112 km) per hour.

Have students name other sea animals and find out how fast they can swim. Make a pictograph on mural paper to show speeds.

Name _____ Date _____

Food Chain

Make an ocean food chain. Read the information about the food chain in the boxes below. Then cut out the pictures along the side of the diagram at the bottom of the page and glue them on the food chain.

Diatoms
One kind of microscopic plant in the sea. Diatoms are the primary source of food for all marine life.

Krill
Small, shrimplike animals that eat diatoms. Krill are eaten directly or indirectly by all other marine animals.

Fish and Squid
It takes large amounts of krill to satisfy the appetites of most fish and squid. Fish and squid graze on the krill all day long.

Seals
Most seals feed on fish and squid that are caught in the cold waters in which the seals swim.

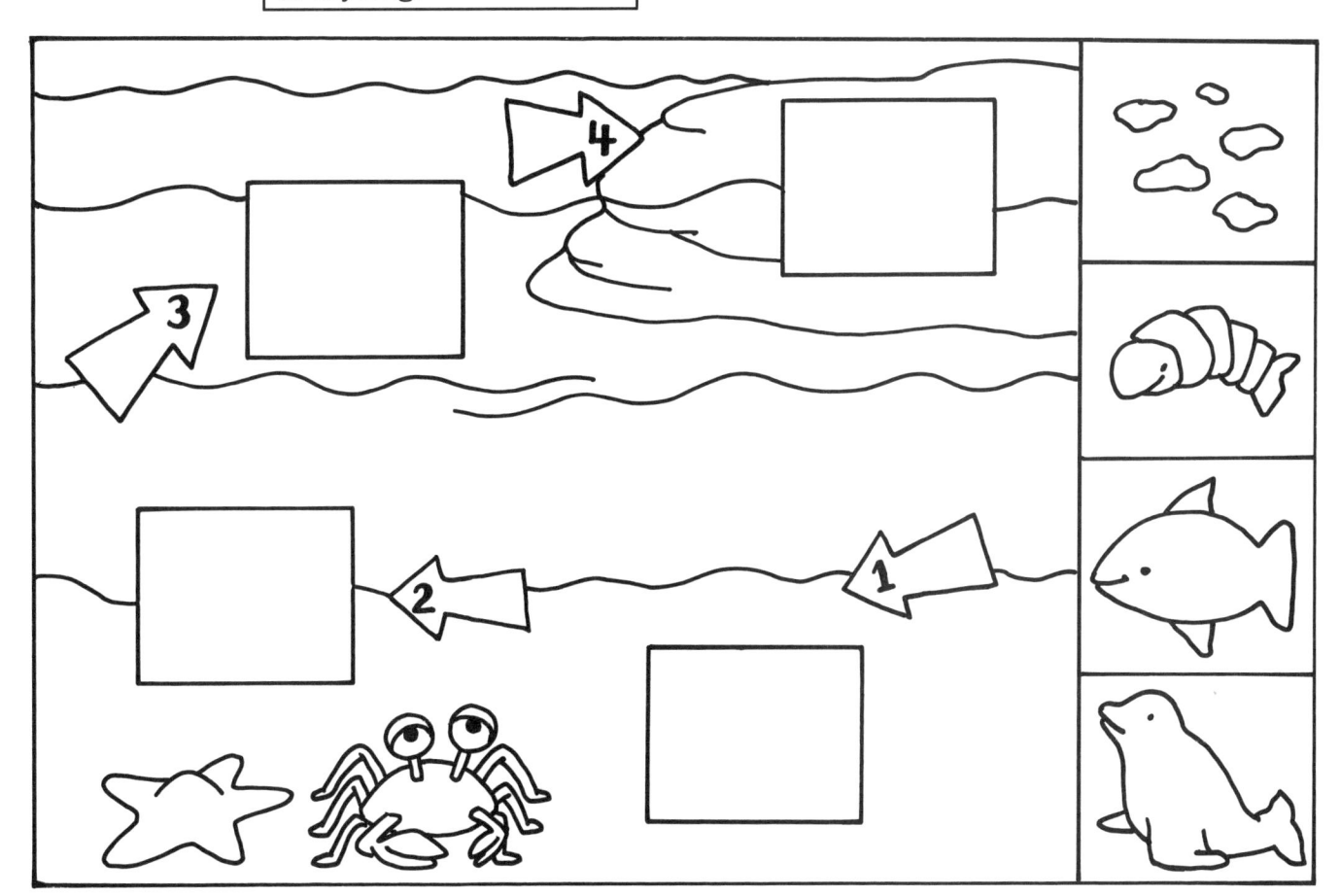

71

© 1992 by Troll Associates.

Records

Sports and Games Records

Share the following sports records with students and have them research others. Allow volunteers to share their findings with the rest of the class. You may wish to use the information here along with the records students find to make a class bulletin board.

Wilt Chamberlain, former basketball player for the Philadelphia Warriors, scored 100 points in a game against the New York Knicks on March 2, 1962. He stills holds the National Basketball Association record for the most points in one game. The record for the most points in a career belongs to Kareem Abdul-Jabbar, who scored 38,387 points from 1969-1989, after which he retired from basketball.

Mark Spitz, an American swimmer, won seven gold medals at the 1972 Olympics. He also set world records in each of these events.

Baseball great Hank Aaron holds the record for the most home runs in a career. With 755, he bettered Babe Ruth's previous record of 714 home runs.

The New York Yankees' first-baseman Lou Gehrig played in 2,130 consecutive baseball games, more than anyone else in the history of the game.

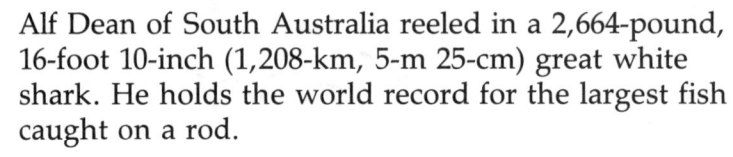

Alf Dean of South Australia reeled in a 2,664-pound, 16-foot 10-inch (1,208-km, 5-m 25-cm) great white shark. He holds the world record for the largest fish caught on a rod.

The highest speed ever reported on a skateboard was 71 mph (114.31 kmph) by Richard K. Brown. The greatest distance for leap-frogging is 888.1 miles (1,430 km), a record set by high school students in New Hampshire in 1988. Also in 1988, a young boy in Colombia set a yo-yo speed record. He made 7,574 loops in just one hour.

While You're at It

Have students try their skill at hula-hooping, leap-frogging, and at making loops with a yo-yo. For each event, post the class records for endurance and for speed. Have students compare their records with the world records. Students who excel in one of these areas may wish to try for a place in the *Guinness Book of World Records*. Display the book to students. They may wish to write to the publisher for more information. Remind students to enclose a self-addressed envelope with their requests.

Guinness Book of
   World Records
Facts on File, Inc.
460 Park Avenue South
New York, NY 10016

World Records for Songs

Survey students to find out what they believe are the three most frequently sung songs. Record each guess on the board. Then have students narrow the three guesses down to *one*.

Begin singing "Happy Birthday to You" and invite students to join in. Then tell students that "Happy Birthday to You" is sung more than any other song in English. It was even sung in space on March 8, 1969 by the astronauts aboard *Apollo IX*. The two other most frequently sung songs are "For He's a Jolly Good Fellow" and "Auld Lang Syne."

Awesome Rap Record

Tell students that Daddy Freddy rapped 507 syllables in sixty seconds on November 24, 1989, beating the world record he set earlier that year with 346 syllables.

Have students write a rap containing at least 500 syllables. Have them practice saying the rap as quickly as possible. Then have "would-be world record holders" rap for the class. Stop them after sixty seconds and have them count the number of syllables they were able to rap in the time allotted. How close did they come to the world record?

Long and Short Notes

A $7\frac{1}{2}$ foot (2.25 m) tall tuba is the world's largest brass instrument. It was constructed for John Philip Sousa.

The largest playable guitar in the world is just over 19 feet (5.7 m) tall.

A drum company in London built the world's largest drum in 1987. It was 13 feet (3.9 m) in diameter.

The smallest playable piano in the world measures $7\frac{1}{2}$ inches × $3\frac{3}{8}$ inches × $6\frac{1}{2}$ inches (19 cm × 9 cm × 16 cm).

73

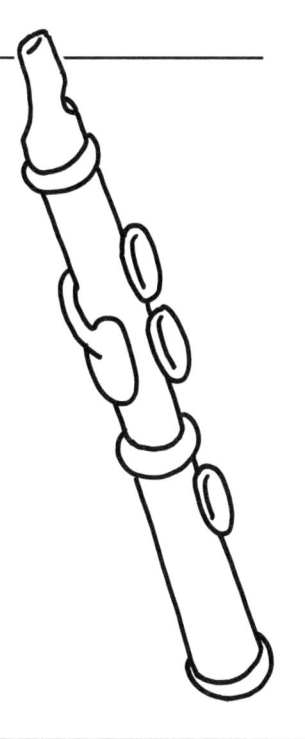

Record Skyscrapers

Explain that the skyline of New York City is dominated by extremely tall office buildings. Tell students that each of the twin towers of the World Trade Center reaches 1,350 feet (411 m) into the air, and each tower has 110 stories. With 102 stories, the Empire State Building stands 1,250 feet (381 m) high. Tell students that the tallest office building in the world is the Sears Tower in Chicago, Illinois. Students will be interested to learn that the Sears Tower has 110 stories that rise to 1,454 feet (443 m). In addition, the building boasts 103 elevators, 18 escalators, and 16,000 windows.

Tall Enough

Make a graph to show the heights of some of the world's tallest structures, including the Sears Tower, the World Trade Center, the Empire State Building, the Eiffel Tower (France), the Great Pyramid of Cheops (Egypt), First Canadian Place (Toronto, Canada), and Mutual Life Citizens (Sydney, Australia). An example follows.

World's Tallest Buildings

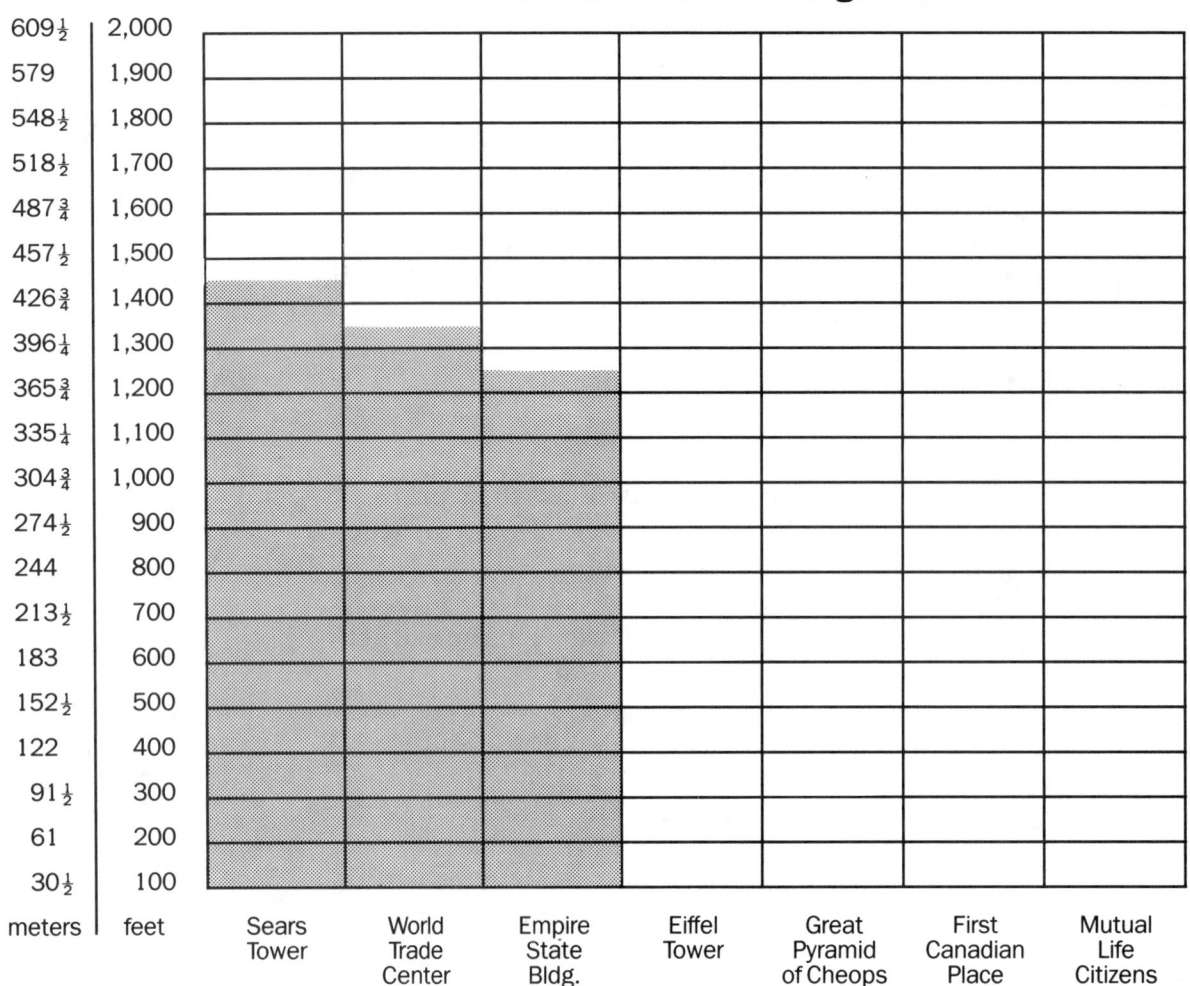

meters	feet	Sears Tower	World Trade Center	Empire State Bldg.	Eiffel Tower	Great Pyramid of Cheops	First Canadian Place	Mutual Life Citizens
609½	2,000							
579	1,900							
548½	1,800							
518½	1,700							
487¾	1,600							
457½	1,500							
426¾	1,400	▓						
396¼	1,300	▓	▓					
365¾	1,200	▓	▓	▓				
335¼	1,100	▓	▓	▓				
304¾	1,000	▓	▓	▓				
274½	900	▓	▓	▓				
244	800	▓	▓	▓				
213½	700	▓	▓	▓				
183	600	▓	▓	▓				
152½	500	▓	▓	▓				
122	400	▓	▓	▓				
91½	300	▓	▓	▓				
61	200	▓	▓	▓				
30½	100	▓	▓	▓				

Making History in a Sailboat

Tell students that an Australian named Sere Testa sailed westward from Brisbane, Australia, through the Panama Canal and then back to Brisbane in 500 days. Testa sailed in *Acrohc Australis*, an 11-foot 10-inch (3.5-m) sailboat, which became the smallest boat to travel around the globe.

Have volunteers track the sea route Sere Testa took on his journey and calculate the number of miles (kilometers) the *Acrohc Australis* sailed.

Fastest Sailboat to Travel Around the World

Explain that Frenchman Philippe Monet set a speed record for sailing around the world in 127 days 12 hours and 11 minutes. Monet made the trip from Brest, France, to Cape Town, South Africa, and then back to Brest in his 75-foot (22.5-m) boat *Kriter Brut de Brut*.

Have volunteers track the sea route Philippe Monet took on his journey and calculate the number of miles the *Kriter Brut de Brut* sailed. Have students use a map or globe to discover shorter routes Monet might have taken and then suggest possible reasons why he traveled what appears to be the long way around.

Plan a Trip

Have students plan their own solo sailboat trip around the world. Write the following topics on the board and have students plan for each. Remind students that the size of the vessel will affect the length of the trip and the amount of the supplies they can pack.

Size of Vessel	Route	Supplies

Ballooning

Closed Balloon

Explain that in 1935, a team of two pilots in a closed balloon set an altitude record of 13.7 miles (22 km).

Open Balloon

In 1957, Major David Simmons set out in an open balloon. Rising to 19.3 miles (30.9 km), he set a height record for an open gondola.

The Master Balloonist

Tell students that Captain Joseph Kittinger is a master balloonist, who, during one flight, set four world records.

World Records #1 and #2

On August 16, 1960, Kittinger put on his flight gear and took off in an open-gondola balloon, called the *Rosie O'Grady*. He rose at least 19.4 miles (31 km) into the air, breaking the world's height records for both manned balloons and for open gondolas.

World Records #3 and #4

At an altitude of 19.4 miles (31 km), Captain Kittinger left the gondola of his balloon and began his record-breaking parachute jump. He fell for 16.2 miles (26 km) before he opened the parachute. When Kittinger reached the ground, he had earned two more world records: the highest parachute jump and the longest free fall.

The *Rosie O'Grady*

Help students to make models of Kittinger's balloon, the *Rosie O'Grady*.

Materials:

papier-mâché mix	balloons	narrow strips of newspaper
tempera and paintbrushes	small plastic fruit baskets	yarn

Help students follow these directions.

1. Blow up and tie a balloon.
2. Dip strips of newspaper, one at a time, into the papier-mâché mixture.
3. Cover the balloon with the moistened strips and let dry thoroughly.
4. Pop the balloon. Paint the papier-mâché to resemble the *Rosie O'Grady*.
5. To make the gondola, weave yarn through the holes in the fruit basket.
6. Punch four small holes near the bottom of the papier-mâché. Use yarn to tie the gondola to the papier-mâché balloon.
7. Hang the balloons in the classroom.

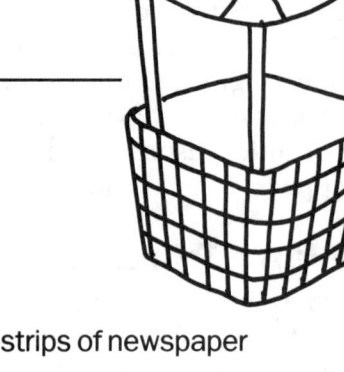

Name _____   Date _____

Decathlon

A *decathlon* is an athletic contest in which each contestant tests his or her skills in ten different events. Plan a decathlon and decide on ten events. You might choose some of the events from an Olympic decathlon, such as running, jumping, and throwing, or you may prefer events more to your own liking, such as jumping rope, throwing a Frisbee, or sack-racing.

Here is what you do.
1. Write the name of each of the ten events in your decathlon.
2. Explain what to do in each event.
3. Decide who will judge the events.
4. Have the contestants perform the events one at a time.
5. Write the names of the events, the names of the contestants, and their best times (allow each contestant to try each event twice) below. Award ribbons to the winners of the events.

Event #1: _____
Contestants/Times:
_____
_____
_____

Event #2: _____
Contestants/Times:
_____
_____
_____

Event #3: _____
Contestants/Times:
_____
_____
_____

Event #4: _____
Contestants/Times:
_____
_____
_____

Event #5: _____
Contestants/Times:
_____
_____
_____

Event #6: _____
Contestants/Times:
_____
_____
_____

Event #7: _____
Contestants/Times:
_____
_____
_____

Event #8: _____
Contestants/Times:
_____
_____
_____

Event #9: _____
Contestants/Times:
_____
_____
_____

Event #10: _____
Contestants/Times:
_____
_____
_____

© 1992 by Troll Associates.

The Solar System

The Starting Lineup
On the chalkboard, draw a diagram of the solar system such as the one below. Discuss with students the relative sizes of the sun and planets. Have students tell what they know about the solar system.

Orbit the Sun
Have students look back at the diagram of the solar system in the previous activity and point out to them that each planet is a different distance from the sun. Ask students which planet orbits the sun in the shortest time. Then ask them which planet takes the longest time to orbit the sun. Help students see that the farther away the planet is from the sun, the longer it takes to orbit the sun. Share the following times with the students and ask them to match each time with the planet to which it refers: 84 years (Uranus), 225 days (Venus), 248 years (Pluto), 12 years (Jupiter), 687 days (Mars), 165 years (Neptune), 365 days (Earth), $29\frac{1}{2}$ years (Saturn), 88 days (Mercury).

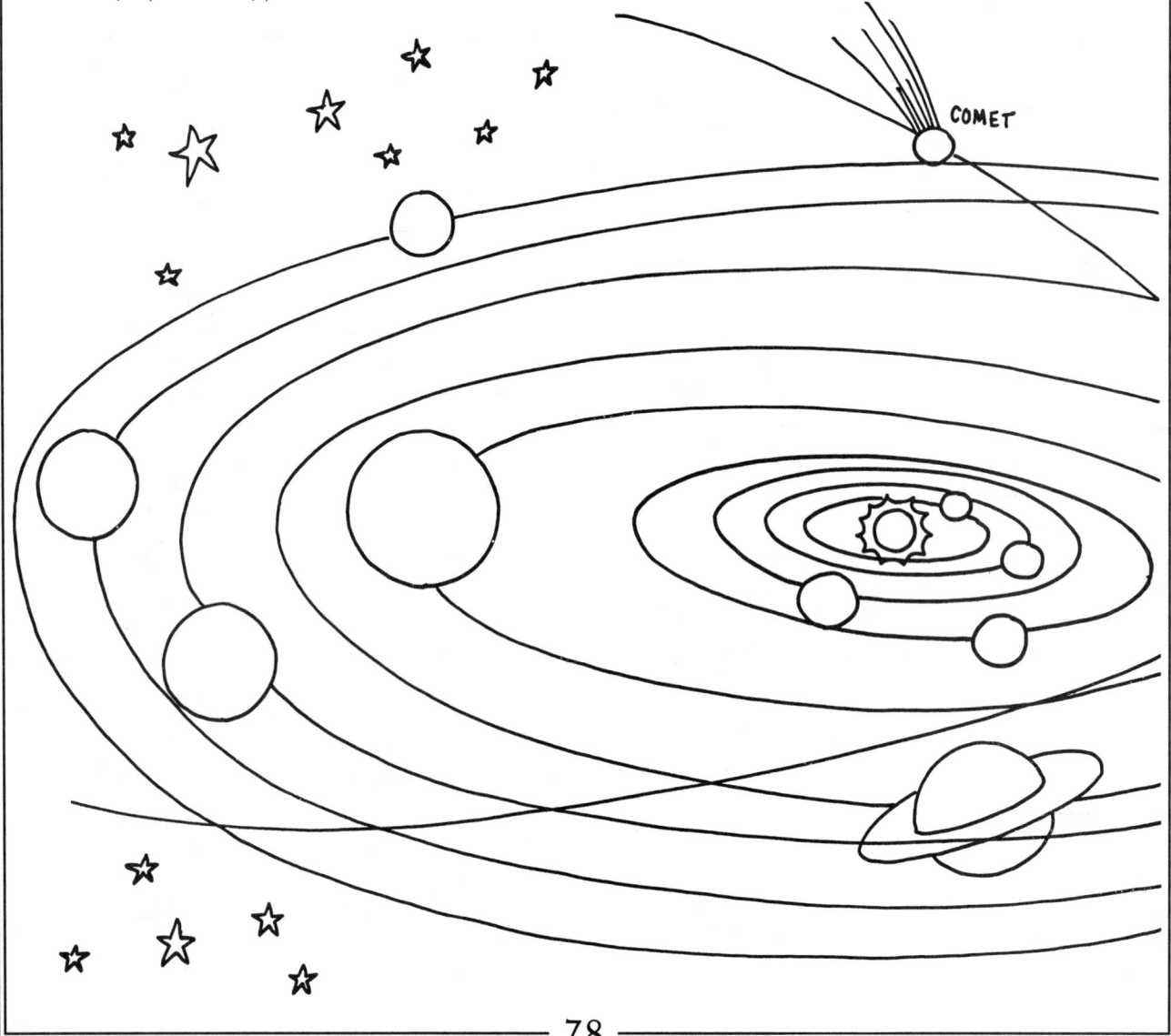

The Sun and Moon

Here Comes the Sun

Explain to students that the sun is a star made up of very hot gases. Tell students that although the sun looks larger than the other stars in the sky, it only *appears* that way because it is much closer to the Earth than the other stars are. Explain that the sun is over 93 million miles (150 million km) from the Earth and that even if it were only 1 million miles (1.6 million km) from the Earth, it would take up nearly the whole sky and cause disastrous effects. Help students perform the following experiment.

PURPOSE: to test the power of the sun
MATERIALS: two chocolate bars, two stones, two apple slices, two pieces of rubber, two sticks of butter, two half-full glasses of water, two half-sheets of newspaper, fourteen index cards
PROCEDURE: On each index card write the name of one object. Place one set of objects along with their cards in the sunniest place in the classroom. Place the other set of objects and their cards in the shadiest place. Tell students to observe each object twice a day for two weeks to learn which objects were most affected by the sun's power. Have students record their observations and any conclusions in their notebooks. Encourage them to share their ideas with their classmates.

Lunar Phases

Tell students that while the Earth revolves around the sun, the moon revolves around the Earth. Point out that because the moon moves around the Earth and has no light of its own, the moon is visible only when it reflects sunlight. Discuss the four lunar phases with students and then ask one student to be the "Earth" and sit on a chair at the front of the room. Ask another student to be the "moon" and stand facing away from the "Earth." Direct the "moon" to move around the "Earth," always facing away from it. Ask students to discuss why it is always the same side of the moon that is visible from the Earth.

The Silent Stones

Display a photograph of the giant stone monuments of Stonehenge in Great Britain. Explain that some scientists believe that Stonehenge was created thousands of years ago by ancient astronomers to study the sun and the moon. In addition, these scientists feel that the stones were used as computing tools to solve mathematical problems associated with astronomy. Have students form small groups to research Stonehenge and speculate on its use.

Comets, Stars, and Falling Stars

Halley's Comet

Explain that scientists sometimes call comets "dirty snowballs" because they are made of a frozen ball of ice covered with thick black dust. Tell students that as a comet nears the sun, the pressure of sunlight moves the dust and causes the comet's glow.

Tell students about British astronomer Edmund Halley and his discovery that the same comet returns to the earth every seventy-five or seventy-six years. Have students research Halley and Halley's comet to find out how this scientist knew that the comet that was sighted in 1531, 1607, and 1682 was one and the same.

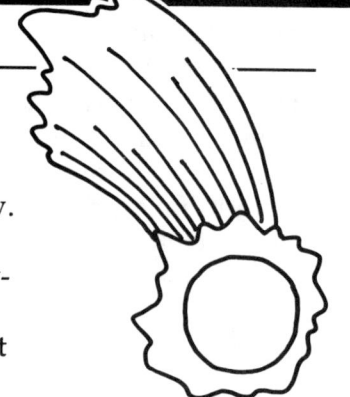

Ancient Stargazers

Tell students that stars are globes of hot gas that range in color from red (the coolest) to blue-white (the hottest). Ask students to conduct a star watch at home, using a tube from a roll of paper towels. Tell students to look through their tubes and observe the night stars at different times on five nights to determine the color of each star. Tell them to record their nightly observations, noting the date, time, weather, and place in the sky where each star appears. Have students share their findings.

The Sky is Falling!

Ask students if they have ever seen a falling, or shooting, star. Explain that these falling objects are not stars at all, but rather flashes or streaks of light caused by tiny grains of cosmic matter that burn up upon entering the earth's atmosphere from outer space. Meteors that reach the earth are called meteorites, most of which are fragments of metal and stone. Display a picture of a meteorite crater and explain that one of the best-known and largest meteorites in the world fell in an Arizona desert and weighed 300 thousand tons (272,158 metric tons)! It made a crater nearly 1 mile (1.6 km) across and 600 feet (183 m) deep. Scientists believe it fell 20,000 years ago.

Constellations

Stars in Your Eyes

Tell students that groups of stars in the sky are called constellations and that constellations seem to form pictures in the sky. Ask students if they have ever been to a planetarium. If so, have them describe their visit. If students are not familiar with a planetarium, explain that it is a building with a dome-shaped ceiling onto which a machine projects an image of the night sky. The image shows how the stars and planets seem to move across the sky. Tell students that some planetariums have ceilings that open so that visitors can observe the sky as a speaker points out various planets and constellations.

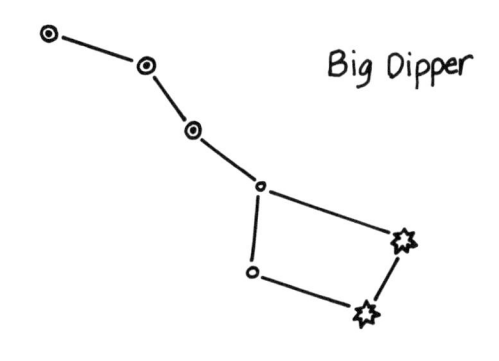

Big Dipper

What Goes on in a Planetarium?

Have students guess the answer to these riddles about the stars.

- What kind of star wears sunglasses? *a movie star*
- Why is Lassie like a comet? *They're both stars with tails.*
- What kind of stars go to jail? *shooting stars*

(The answer to the title is "an all-star show.")

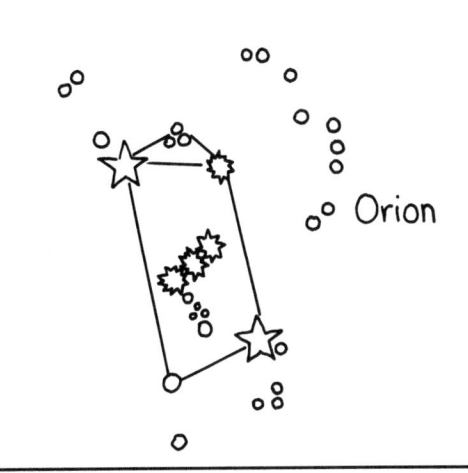

Orion

That's Write!

Have interested students write to one of the following agencies and organizations for more information about constellations:

National Space Society
922 Pennsylvania Avenue, SE
Washington, DC 20024

The Planetary Society
65 North Catalina
Pasadena, CA 91106

Name _____ Date _____

Sunny Side Up

Early peoples learned to harness the sun's power when they made fire using a crude glass lens to concentrate the heat from the sun onto sticks. In the late 1700s, French chemist Antoine Lavoisier invented a device that boiled water using the same principle. Later solar furnaces were redesigned to produce steam, which drives a turbine, which produces electricity. Today solar energy is used to evaporate saltwater so as to extract pure salt to make contaminated water drinkable, and to heat homes and other buildings.

You may find that you use one or more solar inventions in daily life. Look at these pictures of devices that are powered by solar energy and think about how and why they were invented.

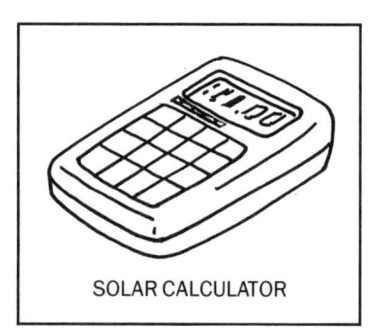

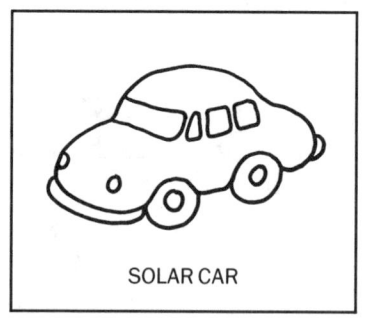

SOLAR CALCULATOR   SOLAR HEAT PANELS   SOLAR CAR

Now invent your own solar-powered device. Design something people all over the world will use. Then draw a picture of your device in the frame. On the lines below explain how your device operates and why it will be popular in the future.

82

© 1992 by Troll Associates.

Name _____ Date _____

Star-ting Over

When you look up into a cloudy sky you may imagine the clouds look like a mermaid or a giraffe. Constellations were named in much the same way.

Look at the groups of stars in each picture and try to imagine a picture. Draw lines that connect the stars to form your imaginary picture. Name each constellation you create and tell why you feel it is the best name.

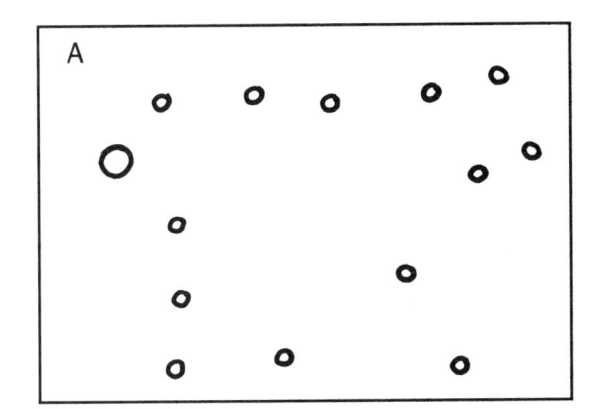

A

Name: _____
_____
_____

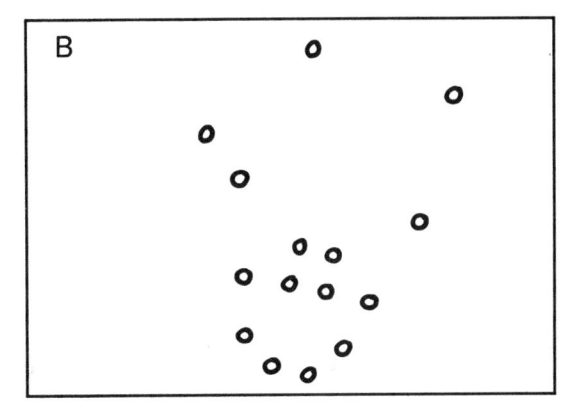

B

Name: _____
_____
_____

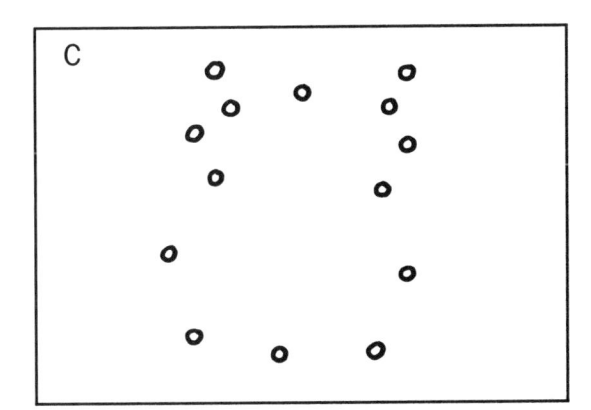

C

Name: _____
_____
_____

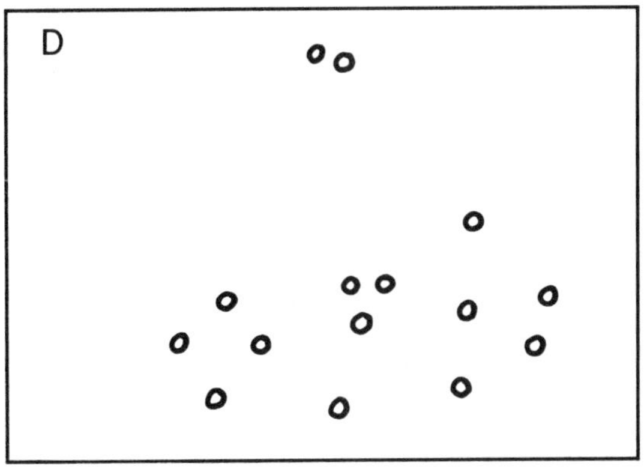

D

Name: _____
_____
_____

83

© 1992 by Troll Associates.

Survival

Coming Out Alive

Tell students that hikers and campers occasionally find themselves in situations in which survival knowledge could save their lives. Ask students what they think are the four basic needs of survival (fire, food, water, and shelter). Pose this problem to students: Pretend you are preparing for a camping trip and want to pack a survival kit. Only ten things will fit into your backpack. What ten items would you take?

Draw a simple outline of a backpack on the board. Have students copy it onto a piece of drawing paper and list the ten items they would choose. When students have finished, take a class poll and post their responses.

Water, Water Everywhere But Never a Drop to Drink

Tell students that water is essential to human survival and that people should drink approximately eight glasses on a regular day and more on a hot day. Explain that hikers and campers should carry their own water on a trip because not all the water they will find outdoors is fit to drink. Share these tips for getting water. Then have students try to think of other tips. Allow them to use reference sources from the library.

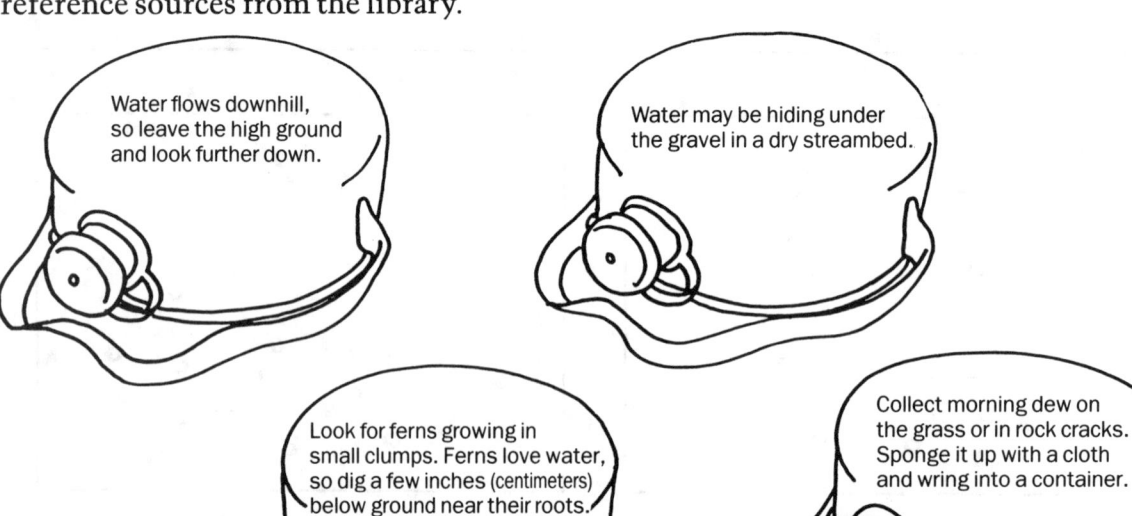

- Water flows downhill, so leave the high ground and look further down.
- Water may be hiding under the gravel in a dry streambed.
- Look for ferns growing in small clumps. Ferns love water, so dig a few inches (centimeters) below ground near their roots.
- Collect morning dew on the grass or in rock cracks. Sponge it up with a cloth and wring into a container.

Hypothermia

Baby, It's Cold Outside!

Explain to students that in wilderness survival, it is important to stay dry and prevent the wind from stealing body heat. Tell them that a condition known as hypothermia may occur when extremely cold air is mixed with high-velocity winds, wetness, and fatigue. Point out that symptoms of hypothermia may include slurred speech, staggering, and shivering. Discuss with students what they should do if a companion exhibits signs of hypothermia. Use the tips below. Then have students form small groups to discuss why each pointer is important.

ALWAYS . . .

prevent further loss of victim's body heat

give the victim a warm, sweet drink

give the victim something sweet to eat

NEVER . . .

try to rub heat into the victim's limbs

use hot water bottles

use fire as a source of heat

Give Me Shelter

Tell students that to guard against hypothermia, a shelter against the cold weather is of prime importance. Explain that shelters can be built in many locations and with a variety of materials. Tell students that people often take shelter in snow caves, beneath downed trees, or beneath overhanging rock ledges.

Now have students design and draw their own shelters.

85

Ecosystems

You Can't See the Forest for the Trees

Tell students that when animals and their habitats form a balanced system, we call that system an *ecosystem*. Explain that the forest is one example of an ecosystem because as trees grow, they drop some or all of their leaves. When the leaves decay, they provide food for the many insects that live on the forest floor. The insects, in turn, provide food for other forest animals. Discuss ways that humans can disturb the forest's ecosystem (cutting down trees for fuel or building houses). Have students make posters to show what people can do to protect the forest and its ecosystem.

Aquasystems

Tell students that aquatic ecosystems face multiple problems, such as water and land pollution caused by industry and agriculture. Discuss with students the kinds of wildlife that are affected by this pollution. Explain that dredging ponds, lakes, and rivers, and filling in land to make way for buildings and roads are two ways these delicate systems are being disturbed. Have students write questions to send to a local industry to learn what is being done to protect the local ecosystem. Invite a representative to visit your class for an interview.

The Desert

Have students brainstorm on the topic of deserts and write their ideas on the board. Display pictures of deserts, showing plant and animal wildlife. Have students discuss how the extraction of natural resources, such as oil, might affect a desert ecosystem. Some students may wish to research the effect of the oil industry on the sands of Saudi Arabia and Kuwait.

The Ozone Layer

Is it Getting Hot in Here?

Remind students that air pollution is a very serious problem. Point out that the atmosphere close to the earth protects those living on it from harmful substances that are in the outer atmosphere. Tell students that one such harmful substance is ultraviolet light. Write "ozone layer" on the board and have students look it up and define it. Help students to understand that the ozone layer is responsible for keeping the earth's immediate atmosphere safe from radiation. Remind students of the sun's blistering heat and ask them to think of problems that might occur if the ozone layer were to be destroyed. Then have them suggest solutions.

Oops, Our Ozone!

Explain that various chemicals used by industries and individuals all over the world, such as aerosol sprays and toxic cleaners, are damaging the ozone layer beyond repair. Have students use old magazines to cut out pictures of products that can harm the ozone layer. Display the pictures on a bulletin board titled "Oops, Our Ozone!"

Pack it Up

Have students take a notebook to the grocery store and copy the address of one or two manufacturers of aerosol products. Then have students write letters to various companies requesting that they stop packaging their product in a way that can harm the ozone layer. Have students share any responses they may receive from the companies.

Respect for Wildlife

Take Refuge

Tell students that today people are more concerned than ever about how to protect wildlife. In the United States and other countries, careful controls are set up to protect wildlife habitats. Tell students that the establishment of national parks, wildlife refuges, and conservation areas have strict rules and regulations prohibiting hunting or otherwise disturbing the wildlife.

Have students use art materials to make signs showing rules that might be posted throughout wildlife preservation areas.

Toad Tunnels

Point out that some people work very hard to preserve balanced ecosystems. As an example, tell students about a toad tunnel that was built under a highway to allow toads access to their breeding ponds without risking their lives to passing vehicles. Have students design a way to protect one form of wildlife that might be endangered due to the clearing of land for farming or industry, the damming of rivers, or the development of mines.

How Can We Help?

Tell students that in 1948, the IUCN, or International Union for Conservation of Nature and Natural Resources, was founded to examine the condition of the world's living resources and to decide which had priority. Explain that without such foundations, many forms of wildlife would die and perhaps become extinct. Point out that much of the funding for the IUCN comes from the World Wildlife Federation, or WWF, whose symbol is the giant panda. Students might be interested to know that there are only about 1,000 giant pandas left in the world today, and that, sadly, they face extinction due to diminishing food sources. Have students find out about the attempts that are being made to prevent the giant panda's extinction and suggest other ways they themselves can help.

Have students bring in a plain white T-shirt (or cut one out of large white construction paper). Supply them with fabric crayons and ask them to design a T-shirt that the IUCN or WWF could use to raise money for conservation projects. Display the T-shirts in the school hallways.

Name _____ Date _____

A Mini Ecosystem

In these boxes, draw pictures of four things you think would grow well in a forest ecosystem you will create.

You will need:
- large jar with lid
- potting soil
- several forest plants, such as ferns, moss, seedling tree
- tweezers or small tongs
- clay
- small sprinkling can
- pencil

To create your ecosystem:

1. Be sure your jar is clean. Ask your teacher to help you punch ten holes into the lid of your jar.
2. Pour potting soil carefully into the jar until it is about one-third full.
3. Decide where you want your first plant to grow and make a shallow hole in the soil with the eraser end of a pencil.
4. With tweezers, carefully pick up the seedling tree and press it into the soil. Use the pencil eraser gently to press down the soil around the seedling's roots.
5. Repeat for each plant in your forest.
6. Make a clay forest animal under your seedling tree.
7. Gently sprinkle your forest ecosystem with water and put on the lid.

© 1992 by Troll Associates.

Whales

A Fish Story?

Ask students what animal ranges from 15 feet (4.6m) to 100 feet (30½m) long, breathes air, can eat up to 4,000 tons (3,629 metric tons) of food a day, and goes on a 6,000-mile (9,656-km) vacation every winter. If students do not guess, tell them that the answer is the whale. Point out that whales are not fish, but mammals—and the biggest mammals that ever lived! Share these other facts about whales with students. Then for each fact have students research the difference between whales and fish.

A Whale Tale

Tell students that hundreds of years ago there were tales of sailors who mistook a sleeping whale for an island. They would anchor their ship near the "island" and "go ashore" to cook their dinner over an open fire. Imagine the sailors' surprise when the whale awakened as it felt the flames upon its back and dived beneath the water, flinging the startled sailors and their dinner into the sea! Have students write an anecdote from the perspective of one of these sailors.

ZIP Code, Please

Tell students that in winter most whales go to warm waters to breed and in summer they return to cold waters to feed. Explain that most whales keep the same migration patterns year after year, which helps scientists to study the same whales for long periods of time. Point out that the humpback whale migrates farther than any other whale, sometimes up to 6,000 miles (9,656 km). Provide research materials so that students can make a map showing the migration routes of the humpback whale.

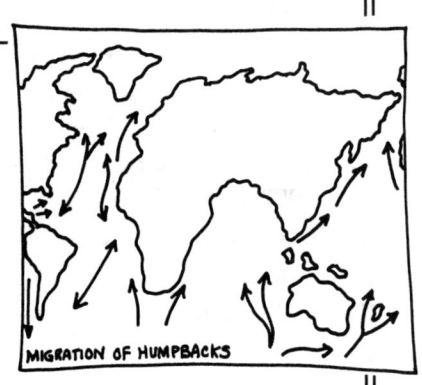

Behavior

Gone Fishing

Tell students that whales need to eat enormous amounts of food. As an example, tell them that the blue whale can eat as much as 4 tons (3.63 metric tons) of food a day!

Tell students that whales have several different ways of feeding, one of which is called "bubble netting." Explain that a humpback swims in a circle below a large school of fish. The whale blows out air, which creates a ring of bubbles that trap the fish. The whale surfaces in the center of the circle with its mouth open and has a feast!

Explain that gray whales stir up the sea bottom with their snouts and suck up the muddy water to "catch" tiny creatures and fish. The whales trap the creatures and fish in their baleen, which are comblike rows of hard fibers in the whale's upper jaw. Baleen strain the food from the water.

Have students write a script for a television show on whales, using some of the above information and whatever else they can find out about how whales feed and what they eat.

Circus Stars of the Deep

Tell students that whales, despite their enormous size, are agile creatures that sometimes perform acrobatic feats. Two such feats are called spy-hopping and breaching. After letting students speculate on the meanings of the terms, explain to them that spy-hopping occurs when a whale holds its body straight up and peeks out of the water. Whales in this position usually extend their flippers and look like they are treading water. Explain that breaching occurs when a whale thrusts its entire body completely out of the water and into the air. Point out that the thunderous splash made as the whale falls back into the water can sometimes be heard over great distances. Have students use library books to find out the lengths and weights of three kinds of whales and find out which can jump the highest.

Communication

Whale Songs

Tell students that nearly all whales sing, but that the most famous whale singer is the male humpback whale, whose songs can be heard for over 20 miles (32 km). Some of the sounds male humpback whales make are the loudest sounds made by any living thing! Explain that these songs can last for up to ten minutes and have parts that repeat. Point out that humpbacks in different areas sing different songs; humpbacks in the cold Pacific do not sing the same songs as those off the Australian coast. Play a recording of whale songs for students and have them listen carefully. Ask students to discuss the sounds and what they think the whales might be trying to communicate.

Echolocation

Tell students that whales do not rely on vision to locate things under water; instead, they use sound. Explain that this method of using sound to locate things is called echolocation. Write the word on the board and have students tell if they recognize two more familiar words in *echolocation*. If necessary, point out the word *echo* and have students define it. Explain that whales make special clicking sounds that bounce off objects, and then the whales listen carefully for the sound waves to echo, or come back to them. In this way the whale can judge how near or far it is from an object and how big or small the object is.

Have students close their eyes as you walk around the room. Tap one student on the shoulder as a signal for him or her to begin tapping with a pencil on a desk. Then let the other students use their listening skills to guess how near or far they are from the person who is tapping.

Touching and Feeling

Since whales do not have hands, they feel things in their environment with their skin. Explain to students that the skin of a whale is much more sensitive than human skin, especially on the head. Tell students that whales, especially mothers and their babies, often touch one another. Have students research the whale's senses and make an illustration to show how whales and humans are similar and/or different.

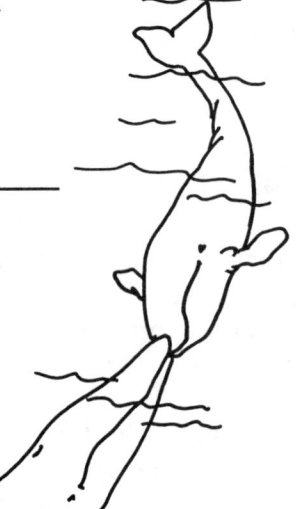

Life Style

A Group of Whales
Tell students that many types of animals, including whales, travel in groups. Have students work in pairs to research pods, or the groups in which whales travel. Have them share their findings with the class.

A Very Special Bond
Tell students that the mother whale takes very good care of her baby. Explain that calves are born with the instinct not to breathe until their blowholes are above the water, so the mother must nudge it to the surface to get its first breath of fresh air. Point out that mother whales are very protective of their young and defend them fiercely if in danger. Some whales have been known to smash boats that have come between them and their calves. Have students discuss the ways whale mothers and human mothers are similar.

World's Biggest Babies
Tell students that newborn whales can be very large. For example, at birth the baby blue whale is longer than a school bus and heavier than an elephant! Share the following table with students to show the size and weight of newborn and adult whales. Then have them research the sizes and weights of other newborn mammals and compare those numbers with the numbers for whales.

Type of Whale	Birth Weight	Birth Length	Adult Weight	Adult Length
Gray Whale	1,500 pounds (680 kg)	15 feet ($4\frac{1}{2}$ m)	90,000 pounds (40,800 kg)	45 feet ($13\frac{3}{4}$ m)
Humpback	1,800 pounds (816 kg)	14 feet ($4\frac{1}{4}$ m)	80,000 pounds (36,287 kg)	50 feet ($15\frac{1}{4}$ m)
Blue Whale	4,400 pounds (1,995 kg)	25 feet ($7\frac{1}{2}$ m)	300,000 pounds (136,077 kg)	90–100 feet ($27\frac{1}{2}$–$30\frac{1}{2}$ m)
Fin Whale	3,600 pounds (1,633 kg)	21 feet ($6\frac{1}{2}$ m)	140,000 pounds (63,503 kg)	88 feet (27 m)

Endangered Whales

The Whaling Industry

Explain to students that about three hundred years ago, hunting whales became big business. Hundreds of thousands of whales were hunted nearly to extinction! Tell students that before commercial whaling began, scientists estimated that there were 115,000 humpbacks in the world's oceans, but now there are only about 10,000. Ask students to make posters to educate the public about the plight of whales if commercial whaling is not halted.

A World Without Whales

Tell students that whalers were the first people to notice that some types of whales were disappearing, because they were having a hard time finding humpbacks, blues, and sperm whales to hunt. In 1911, a British museum called for scientific research on the mass killing of whales in the Antarctic Ocean, but the research did not stop the slaughter because such slaughter was highly profitable. Tell students that the greatest hope for saving the whales came in 1946 with the establishment of the IWC, or the International Whaling Commission, whose purpose was to protect the future of the whales. One species after another was given protection, and one country after another gave up commercial whaling. Finally, in 1986, after years of hard work and much opposition, a moratorium on whaling began. All commercial whaling ended in 1988.

Save the Whales!

Tell students that environmental action groups have been organized to inform the public about their causes. Explain that such groups often use pressure tactics to stir up publicity. One of the tactics these groups used to end whaling was to position themselves in boats (often inflatable) on the ocean between the whaling ship and the whale. Point out that members of Greenpeace hoped that the gunner on the whaling ship would be unable to fire at the whale, thereby saving its life. Explain that other groups have gone even further than Greenpeace and have actually sunk whaleboats and destroyed whale processing plants on shore. Have students discuss the effectiveness of each tactic.

Scrimshaw

Eskimos used to carve delicate designs called scrimshaw on whalebone or whale teeth. Soon sailors on long whaling trips were carving scrimshaw. The technique was simple, but it took a lot of time. The tooth or piece of bone had to be carefully cleaned and polished. Then the sailors used a jacknife or sharpened nail to scratch the drawing into the bone. If the sailors were not good artists, they pasted a picture on the bone and traced over it with the knife. When the carving was complete, the sailors filled in the lines with black soot from a lamp and then polished the carving.

Scrimshaw was made illegal in an effort to protect whales. Most scrimshaw today is found only in museums. In the frame below draw a simple scene you might have carved in scrimshaw if you were a sailor on a whaling ship. Then use a sharp pencil to carve your design into a bar of white soap. Rub some black tempera into your carving to make it complete.